**CURIOUS
CREATIVE
CONNECTED**

To Ed,
I hope some of the ideas
here inspire yet more
brilliance in your life.
Best wishes,

Alex.

CURIOUS
CREATIVE
CONNECTED

Engaging Human Intelligence
in a Tech-driven World

ALEX PEARSON

Edited and produced by: Deborah Taylor, Book-Launch Your Business
https://www.booklaunchyourbusiness.com

Original text design by: Joanne Lloyd
https://www.joannelloyd.net

Page design and layout by: Catherine Williams
https://www.chapter-one-book-production.co.uk

Cover design: Andy Prior
http://andypriordesign.co.uk

ISBN: 979-8-6816875-0-4

Contents

Why Human Intelligences?

'It looks as if there were a single ultimate goal for mankind, a far goal toward which all persons strive. This is called variously by different authors self-actualization, self-realization, integration, psychological health, individuation, autonomy, creativity, productivity, but they all agree that this amounts to realizing the potentialities of the person, that is to say, becoming fully human, everything that person can be.'　　　　—Abraham Maslow

TECHNOLOGICAL INNOVATION IS CHANGING LIVES. Take 21-year-old Mike. He banks online, streams videos on demand, communicates with his friends via thumb power, orders food deliveries through an app, registers his bus ticket by QR code, checks his heartbeat, turns his heating up, swipes left and, on occasion, right. He applies for jobs by creating and uploading a video explaining his unique selling points, passes online psychometric tests and interacts in a virtual interview. He buys products that are constructed purely by machines, he books a telemedicine appointment to see his doctor, and creates music through a synthesiser while jamming with friends in five different cities. His life is rich with creativity and connectivity, much of it made possible through technological innovations. The work that Mike will eventually do will be cognitive and creative, the kind of work that only humans can do.

This human-centred work is not just for those entering the workforce in the coming years; the working landscape is changing for everyone, whatever their age, whatever their profession. Anything that can be automated is becoming so, such is the creative drive of the technological revolution. And as machines and algorithms take over the more automatable jobs, it is imperative that we, as human beings, focus our efforts and learning opportunities on developing and harnessing the most human of skills: curiosity, creativity and the ability to connect with others.

This is because we have a distinct advantage over machines. We have the ability to imagine, to dream of a future, to aspire to change and make that change happen. While machines are certainly part of the positive disruption in almost all industries, they lack the ability to imagine. Machines are, by all accounts, efficient and productive, but they can't even begin to compete with humans in our capacity to envision, to fabricate and to perceive future opportunities. Some industries are going crazy for machine learning, but robots cannot replicate human intelligence or replace humans. Robots and algorithms are restricted to their specific sphere, to do what they are programmed to do. A data collection system programmed to support your online shopping experience cannot suddenly imagine a new product, it can merely inform you of the data it is collecting. A robot serving food in a restaurant does not want to play the piano when it is off duty. Machines are built for specific purposes.

Technological advances can bamboozle. Their functions astonish. But amongst the development and implementation of all this clever technology there is a danger that the workforce will be seen as part of the mechanical process. It's too easy to forget that a team comprises thinking, feeling beings. An overuse of – and over reliance on – technology can leave team members stranded on isolated islands, forming restricted silos of expertise. As such, they have little hope of meaningful connection or communication with others, and even less hope of a cross-fertilisation of ideas. It's the human connection across silos – the exchange of ideas and expert knowledge – that makes space for and gives opportunity for creative breakthroughs. It is also where we feel good. But if we are so in awe of technological potential that we forget our people, we dissolve that innovative opportunity like salt in water.

Seeing customers as just a number on a profit and loss sheet, rather than human beings with needs and desires, brings its own dangers. The world loves machine learning. But is it sustainable to ask the customer to be patient while he or she teaches the machine? I had this experience very recently when I tried to get help solving a technical problem with the software I was using. I got onto the online chat that was offered on the homepage, but I just kept receiving endless apologies: 'I am sorry, I didn't quite understand that', 'Forgive me, I am learning', 'Can you use other words to describe your request?', 'Sorry, could you try and be more specific in your description? I am learning'. I never did get an answer to my quite simple question because I failed to teach the machine what the problem was in the first place!

Do you feel there's a need to balance the use of digital technology with the fostering of human intelligence in all organisations, large and small?

If you're part of an organisation that uses technology to promote flexible, forward-looking, constructive working conditions, you no doubt feel empowered and want to contribute and grow. If you're a member of an organisation that tries to place you within the automation process, making no separation between you as a human and the demands of the machine, then you're likely to feel dehumanised and void of dignity and respect.

We must try to prioritise the capacity and needs of the human workforce in a world dominated by digital and technological progress. This doesn't mean reducing the use of technology – whether you're an individual or an organisation it's there to help you after all – but it does mean placing more emphasis on, and making more time for, nurturing different aspects of human intelligence to ensure you're in charge of technology rather than being a slave to it.

We all want to live in a world that is future-focused, hopeful, compassionate and creative. These are human qualities born of curiosity and nurtured through connection with others. The technology just does the hard work.

The Future of Skills

It's important to acknowledge that technological innovation only exists in the realm of the human imagination. It takes a human mind to envisage the future, imagine potential and visualise cutting edge outcomes. These creative skills are specific to people – it is merely the automated outputs that are transmitted by robots, machines and algorithms.

But, of course, it's not just digital transformation that is carving out the future of work. We must also consider the changing attitudes of people across the world. Our Anthropocene (human-focused) era is pushing the planet ever closer to it limits. We are awakening to new innovations and industries in green technology, health care and environmental protection. There is a burgeoning demand for predictions of natural disasters, so responses can be actioned faster. Just as our great grandparents could hardly imagine space travel, we can hardly imagine the inventions and interventions of the coming decades. But we would be wise to prepare.

Curious, Creative, Connected

The landscape of the future of work is already changing, and this has substantial implications for the skillsets that are needed moving forward. According to a 'Future of Skills' report by Pearson and Nesta, the skills that will be in greater demand include 'interpersonal skills, higher-order cognitive skills, and systems skills'. These are human intelligences founded on key capacities of curiosity, creativity and connectedness, the chosen areas of discussion for this book.

Curiosity

The first of the human intelligences (or capacities) under discussion is curiosity, which prepares you to be open to new ideas. Curiosity nurtures the 'yes and' response rather than 'yes but' and keeps thinking divergent, open and exploratory, while also keeping judgement at bay. On an organisational level, the spacious inquisitiveness of curiosity can lead to new discoveries as well as new approaches to processes, models, values and strategies.

Curious thinking is also thoughtful and deliberate. It's about challenging and questioning, being observant and attentive to detail. As a friend in a leadership role put it to me: 'Curiosity is a responsibility, it is a leadership ethic. A leader has a primary need to be curious, to do the right things.'

On an individual level curiosity is about personal growth. Being the nucleus of your internal reward system, curiosity increases your ability to build strong relationships and to self-manage. It also drives you to explore, learn and reflect. Furthermore, it marks the beginning of your creative process.

Creativity

Creativity is fundamentally about creating new ways of looking at, thinking about and being in the world. With the avalanche of new technologies, new business models, and new socio-geopolitical challenges, creative thinking is now a skill in top demand. Creative problem solving is a highly sought-after skill, whether for dealing with a customer service procedure, product development and strategy design for improving current internal processes.

Creativity also develops confidence, stamina and determination. Creative teams thrive on ambiguity and move effortlessly between divergent exploratory thinking and convergent analytical thinking. Creative individuals thrive in adversity, they reframe challenges into opportunities and look for solutions in the deepest of trenches.

Connected

Finally, we contemplate an holistic understanding of connectedness. Connectedness feeds our souls: as individuals, teams, organisations and societies. It is the most desired of all human needs: to belong, to share, to grow together. It starts with a connection to self, an awareness of your own strengths and desires, and an ability to self-manage. But it is also about the connection to others that allows you to build strong and authentic bonds with those around you.

Connected teams are authentic in their communication and principled in their actions. Connected individuals are self-aware and content. But connectedness also goes beyond you and your community. It nudges you to an awareness of your connection to the world in which you live, creating a sense of pleasure in serving a higher purpose.

Each of these human intelligences comprise skills, behaviours and attitudes that can be developed over time, with patience and practice. And in the coming chapters we will explore methods for building cognitive muscle on both the individual and team level.

As you will see, these human intelligences are collaborative and transferable. They help intertwine previously diverse concepts and ideas in original ways to create unique products and processes. And they add magic to every industry. Clara uses her creativity to remanufacture sportswear out of old fishing nets. Jane, driven by her curiosity, challenges the status quo of old-fashioned accounting and combines technology with imagination to benefit her customers. Veronica, globally connected, extends her diplomatic ties and collaborates across borders often without leaving her flat in east London. Peter brings new ideas of organisational structuring from previous collaborations into his health care work.

Human intelligences will always surpass artificial intelligences of any type. They apply to everything from butchering and baking to candlestick making. They are consignable skills; human operating systems. They can be learned, practiced and mastered then applied to everything, be it accounting, law, product design, e-commerce, social and health care or manufacturing. More than anything else they help you imagine the future.

Curiosity creates compassion, which stokes the desire to take action to improve the lives of others. This allows for win-win growth and promotes a culture of inquiry and questioning, rather than one of defensive reactionary responses.

Creativity takes courage as well as the ability to see failure as growth and mistakes as opportunities on which to unleash creative potential.

Essential to creativity is agility, the ability to move fast and change direction swiftly, creating opportunity from change. As Michael Arena, Vice President for Talent and Development at Amazon Web Services puts it, agile organisations require manoeuvrable and autonomous 'speed boats' or small teams of diverse expertise that are interdependent in nature and can dash off and experiment in the choppy waters of change while the mothership manages the macro level organisational needs. This requires strategic thinking and flexibility around team structure. And the speed boats need to be strategically dispatched as there is little sense in launching off the port side if the opportunities are starboard.

Connection to others is built on trust and trustworthiness, which creates strong bonds, powerful teams and open communication that supports successful teamwork. Meanwhile, collaboration uses individual strengths to create team greatness by tapping into and valuing diversity.

Creating Your Future

While writing this book, I interviewed several people from many different industries to assess current attitudes to the application of human intelligences at work. My interviews included a senior analyst at a large American bank, a senior executive at a Fortune 500 company, the general manager of a hotel chain, two academics in higher education, a senior civil servant and several successful entrepreneurs working in diverse spaces, such as green energy, tech and the circular economy.

I also interviewed middle managers in large organisations to try to understand whether, even if the top level believes in it, human-centred leadership and support for human intelligences cascaded down throughout the organisation. I asked whether employees felt they were able to truly engage their full potential to work towards the common goal. Many responses support my argument that more effort, more time and more focus is needed to nurture human intelligences throughout organisations, both large and small.

This book provides a road map to engage your human intelligences of curiosity, creativity and connectedness so you can respond to change in a positive and purposeful way. The book focuses on putting human intelligence at the core of individual, team and organisational growth. It's a handbook for building the skills and mindsets that can secure a rich future – one that not only keeps pace with change but that cherishes the space for new opportunities.

This book is for leaders looking for inspiration on how to prepare their team for a future of change and opportunity and who see their people as the key to forging a positive, purposeful future. It's also for individuals who want to foster human connectedness in a world of digital realism and ongoing social transition and who cherish the human aspect of the creative process.

The concepts discussed in the following pages will hopefully open your mind to new ideas, approaches and attitudes to working in this new era. They'll take you on a journey where curiosity, creativity and connectedness help you gain confidence and take ownership of your contribution to your work, your organisation, your colleagues and to the world. The intention is to help you find ways to make small changes that deliver big results for you, your team and the community in which you live.

I hope it will become part of your story of gaining autonomy and motivation that allow you to generate creative outcomes and connection to yourself, to others and to the world in which we all live.

Chapter 1:

Change is Upon Us ... and That's a Good Thing

Our lives and work are being profoundly altered by modern technology. Mostly, this is positive, with automation doing away with many laborious and monotonous jobs. But there is another side to the picture, and ethical questions are now being raised about how some new technologies impact our global society and the health of our planet.

Change and The Future of Work

OVER THE PAST THREE DECADES, our global society has witnessed monumental shifts in lifestyles and working patterns. Innovation, global trade, social transition, war and even plague have been changing society for some 2.5 million years, since stone tools were invented and we shifted to a more sedentary lifestyle. But the melding of population increase, globalisation, digital and internet innovations together with technological transformation has exponentially accelerated the rate of change.

Let's go back just a few decades to hear an interesting tale of how just one technological innovation transformed a society in the short space of 40 years. Since the late 1980s, China leapt from being a country with very limited telecommunications to one with ultra-sophisticated mobile technology.

As an extension of this development, many large cities, like Beijing, Shanghai and Shenzhen became almost entirely cashless. Now, China is a country where all people of all ages have to adapt to using mobile technology. Even the sweet potato street vendors use a QR code to collect payment through mobile technology.

In fact, everything is done through a wireless device – online shopping, ordering a taxi, paying bills, dealing in stocks and shares, and managing deliveries. In January 2020, all Chinese citizens were required to download and use a tracing app to facilitate free and safe movement within cities and towns to keep the coronavirus at bay.

Spurred on by the digital disruption, the employment landscape of China has utterly changed. Since the late 1990s, industry started to focus on the development of infrastructure, high-tech manufacturing, AI surveillance systems and alternative energy technology. All of this created a booming tech sector which, since 2015, has generated over one million new high-tech jobs annually. But other industries have faced a different fate and while China is still considered a global manufacturing hub, automation has brought about job displacement on an enormous scale.

Closer to home, the employment landscape in Europe is also altering rapidly. Research indicates that 65% of children under five will work in jobs that have yet to be created. Although we don't know exactly what these jobs will look like, it's possible to predict a key shift in emphasis in these roles. Due to the reliance on technology and the current day speed of change, the skills needed will be more and more around creativity, problem solving and agile decision making.

The impact of the technological transformation means the jobs of the future – as well as many roles in existence today – will require employees to have the ability to work with data. And specifically, to be able to collect and analyse huge chunks of digital information for use in every process, from business development to healthcare management. Added to that, these roles will call for several advanced soft skills, including that of active listening, the ability to monitor oneself and others, the social skills of persuasion and emotional intelligence, and the aptitude for teaching and coaching others.

Technological Innovations and Change

So, it is becoming more and more apparent how our lives are being profoundly altered by the emergence of modern technology. Mostly, those changes are positive. Today, a virtual and global business approach is not only affordable, but doable due to cloud computing, virtual communication technologies and new working patterns. Technology is challenging the status quo and the established role of the office space is shifting.

But with the outbreak of the coronavirus in spring 2020, many businesses were forced to adjust to remote working across teams, cities and countries – something that wouldn't have been possible without technological development. Start-ups and small businesses tapped into expertise from all over the world by building virtual teams, because business information technology granted them instantaneous communication.

Industries and institutions have been heading towards virtual working for years, but the virus pushed businesses and organisations to adapt at high speed. Entrepreneurs and large establishments alike were edged into change, ready or not. As organisations adapted to the new normal, an emerging market of companies using new technologies like Zoom Inc, fought for customers and market share.

It isn't just business that's benefitting from digital technology. Many laborious, repetitive and sometimes dangerous work has been made much easier by technical innovation. Everything from vacuum cleaners and washing machines to tunnelling equipment and sky-skimming cranes. Automation expedites and eases a great number of laborious procedures that previously required hours of manual, often monotonous work.

New computer programmes and mobile apps have transformed industries like banking and tax reporting, saving time, money and in many cases a lot of grief. These innovations, while streamlining organisational systems, have also cost jobs, although the world of work is also busy creating new jobs, as we will see a little later. The digital and technological revolution has truly transformed how almost all organisations operate and there are few that would dispute the positive progression. But for all the benefits, there are disadvantages to all this change too.

It's impossible to look at the positive changes without considering the impact it has had on society as a whole. Organisations are using technology to enable life-changing opportunities such as using artificial intelligence to thwart large-scale criminal activity. Others are developing robotics that offer amputees intricate movement through highly sophisticated artificial limbs. Micro finance systems are fostering entrepreneurship that is pulling millions out of poverty in developing countries through the roll out of The Internet of Things, and other inspiring companies are saving lives by building affordable and replicable 3D printed lifesaving gear. Heightened airport security following the 9/11 attacks saw the introduction of Advanced Imaging Technology (AIT) and millimetre wave body scanners that use electromagnetic waves to scan passengers for unusual objects on their body.

Contact tracing is being used by some countries in the wake of the coronavirus using a mixture of technologies including geo-spatial, machine learning, big data and artificial intelligence. Commercial satellites now offer high-resolution imagery that facilitate pollution detection, deforestation and other climatic change. Suffice to say that the technological transformation is hugely beneficial on many levels and in many arenas.

There is another side to the picture though, and the

darker side is worth considering when thinking about the future of work. Ethical questions are being raised about the development, application and usage of a selection of new technologies. Some innovations aim to extend life, others to offer high speed travel, yet others to enable instantaneous delivery of information and goods, but at what cost? And while the world is generally becoming more secure, supported in part by the use of technology, it is also becoming harder to secure.

In many organisations, digital technology is changing the face of work. It offers progress, that's undeniable, but it also gives rise to huge uncertainty and anguish for many people about the future of work. Many roles that exist today probably won't exist in 20 years from now. That makes it hard to know which new skills you and all your team need to learn now to be confident of employment in the future. How do you maintain a sense of autonomy in a world of data collection and surveillance?

The key is in balancing human intelligence with technological intelligence. In this brave new world of digital enlightenment, each one of us needs to build the skills and mindset to ensure a rich future where we work with technology, not against it. It's only by doing this that we'll be able to create projects, businesses and organisations that are purposeful and create a sense of value for all stakeholders.

Future of Work

So, what impact do all these changes, good and bad, have on the future working landscape? A good place to start is by acknowledging the way in which huge numbers of jobs disappear due to the introduction of process technology. So while jobs are disappearing in banking, accounting and manufacturing (to name but a few), they are being reborn in even larger numbers elsewhere, although with entirely new job specifications.

Shorthand typists. Tram drivers. Switchboard operators. Rat catchers. Milkmen. Human alarm clocks. These are but a few examples of roles that barely exist anymore. What did all these people do when personal computers became affordable, trams were replaced by traffic jams, switchboards moved to the cloud and online shopping became the norm?

In 1945, the UK navy employed 861,000 people. In 1970, it was 86,000 and in 2017 it dropped again to 29,280. Kodak was established in the 1880s and by the 1950s had 70% of the market share for amateur camera film. But when digital cameras (ironically designed by one of their own engineers) came onto the scene in the 1980s, Kodak were slow to change. What Kodak failed to grasp was the changing attitude to photography. It was no longer simply about preserving memories by creating an archive, it was about sharing experiences. Kodak filed for bankruptcy in 2012, but in 2013 it emerged from bankruptcy and began focusing on digital imaging and print technology instead. It now partners with cutting edge companies across the globe to produce tablets, phones and specialist movie film.

What has happened to bank clerks, makers of compact disks and vinyl since the advent of online banking and mobile streaming? What happened to the 120,000 odd employees of

Kodak? Resilient people and organisations retrained, found new directions, upskilled and changed.

It's no different now, except the speed of change has accelerated. About a third of the jobs that currently exist will not exist in the year 2030. It's likely that a staggering 80% won't exist by 2040 and yet we don't know what new careers will appear to replace them. What's interesting is that some extinct jobs are making a comeback. With the new awareness of consumption, public health and climate change roles such as that of a milkman is returning. Other industries will change unrecognisably, as did Kodak and so too with the related and accompanying jobs. Digital innovation has created a world of change, full of opportunity and possibility. But one that also brings new challenges and new needs for personal and professional skill sets.

Organisational change has perhaps had the biggest impact on employees. But change is happening so fast that teams hardly have time to adjust to one alteration before another one comes along. So, resilience and agility become crucial skills for helping organisations adapt and thrive.

People want to create, they feel empowered when they do, and they want to own their creations. This is the new way – the way demanded by employees of today. So now, more than ever before, leadership is about recruiting for diversity, judging for curiosity and coaching team members to release their real potential within organisations. It's all about people power.

This process of empowering people leads to growth. But individuals need to feel confident that they have the skills to move seamlessly forward in their career. And they need to feel assured their employer has the right setup in place to help them achieve their goals. That means the organisation needs the culture, values, shared sense of purpose and direction, and a powerful strategic roadmap that considers process, purpose and people to support all stakeholders in succeeding.

If you currently hold in a sales position in your organisation, you might already feel that skillsets are shifting. Modern-day sales tasks are more and more reliant on the capability of collecting and analysing data. So, great salespeople of the future will need to develop strong aptitudes for systems evaluation. This will enable them to better understand their audiences, so they can design sales targets accordingly, as well as monitor subtle shifts in consumer behaviour and adapt their plans where necessary.

Do you work in trade? As trade shifts to a more global outreach with customers across continents, having international communication skills – which include an awareness of cultural intelligence and a global service orientation that takes into account cultural differences – are becoming key skillsets. If you work in the technical field, then fluency of ideas and originality are going to be vital as innovations come in thick and fast, so being able to make connections and act quickly becomes paramount in order to stay ahead of the curve. The future of administration is also looking different. It's likely to become increasingly focused on coordination and operation analysis as well as the ability to make fast and good judgements and decisions.

Managers of the future will need new skills too. For example, they'll need to know how to tackle systems analysis and be creative, curious and open minded. They'll also need to be effective managers of diversity and be capable of responding quickly to change. And, according to a Pearson forecast for 2030, if you're a leader, you'll need to have the ability to think globally, act locally and be focused on a human-centred approach.

Do these predicted changes to your skills requirements send you into spasms of despair or bring you energy and hope? There's always great uncertainly about what the future will bring in terms of organisational structure, roles and processes. However, one certainty remains. Positions, titles, expectations and requirements are going to change. As they say, change is the only constant.

The Modern Need for Lifelong Learning

For the first time ever, the age range of employees within larger companies and organisations now spans five generations. This is big news for both employees and employers, as well as entrepreneurs. According to research, the expected lifespan of those born in the 1940s is 74. For those born in the 1950s and 1960s it rises to 94. For those born after the year 2000 it's a whopping 104. That means young people starting university in the 2020s are expected to live for more than 100 years.

Of course, there are discrepancies in these figures. For example it's widely acknowledged that the less privileged aren't hitting these targets, which is a debate in itself. But, nevertheless, there are huge implications in these figures.

The orthodox life-model, which has been in existence since the industrial revolution, is divided into three parts: education (3 to 23 years), work (23– 65 years) and retirement (65 -75 years). Education has traditionally been seen as preparation for a particular career in a certain industry. Whilst this may have been appropriate for the 1930s (and a world before the huge social and political changes brought about by digital technology), the model is no longer fit for purpose. Retiring at 70 will soon be the norm, but even then, it's likely that many will have another 20 years or more to pay for. And not only pay for, but to be a part of, engaged in and useful in. After all, they'll still be in a position to share decades of knowledge and experience for the betterment of society.

Lynda Gratton's perception-changing book *The 100-year Life* explores a possible new approach and deviates from the traditional three-stage model. In her book she proposes maybe four or five stages of life. These include additional periods of exploration and education because it's unlikely that the skills you learnt in your twenties will keep you in employment (and satisfied) throughout your life.

Enter adult learning. Here, in the world of lifelong learning, lies your opportunity to bring skills up to date, develop new interests and recreate past experiences into new expertise. There is a whole industry formed around the principles of adult learning, both face to face and online, and it runs parallel to the constant changes in organisational structure, processes and purpose. At the core of adult education is self-directed learning; autonomous and self-governed learning journeys built around individual beliefs, values and purpose. The learning must be relevant and meaningful, goal-oriented and practical with tangible benefits and outcomes. It must be intrinsic in its motivational appeal, linked closely to each individual's sense of personal development. And perhaps most important of all, it should raise past experiences to new heights, allowing for the sharing of expertise, know-how and wisdom.

It's becoming clear that retraining and upskilling is now central to keeping motivated and employed in the new scheme of longevity. What will your contribution be to the world in your 80s – and how will you best share your decades of experience and knowledge? What does your lifelong learning journey look like?

Balancing Human Intelligence

Organisations need to build agile, resilient, innovative and engaged teams to successfully navigate ongoing change. Teams need to work collaboratively to make connections between previously disjointed ideas and to think holistically about the future. Smart organisations build the ability to combine cross-sector thinking, to graft the creatives with the techies, the systems thinkers with the design scholars and to look for solutions in a non-traditional fashion. Future-focused businesses build resilience on an individual and organisational level to properly support and manage change, to convert anxiety and stress to optimism and hope.

Organisations call for agile and supple teams that can respond quickly to rapid shifts in the marketplace. Perhaps most important of all is that organisations should strive to build teams that are engaged. Teams that feel integral to the organisation's mission and comprise individuals that feel confident in their contribution to the team's output.

All of these are built through fundamentally human skills with the intelligences of curiosity, creativity and connectedness at the foundation of all these capabilities. They are transferable across sectors and lie at the very heart of personal and professional growth.

Fostering human intelligence in tandem with technological transformation puts individuals and teams in the driving seat, converting digital and technological innovations into tools not traps. Nurturing purpose-driven teams within an organisation that puts social and environmental values on a par with profit creates powerful activists who are driven to do their best to meet the common goal. Embedding human intelligence into the organisational change methodology is conducive to future success.

How This Book Can Help

In the following chapters you will learn how to develop human intelligences in order to build resilience, agility and innovative thinking in your business or career. This approach aims to put you in the driving seat of the technological transformation and to prepare you fully for the future of work. You'll discover tools and techniques to foster empathy and build strong and collaborative teams; teams that use machines but empower people to steer the organisation to success.

_____

Chapter 2

Curiosity

Cited as being dangerous, childish, even superfluous, curiosity is anything but. It is the bedrock of learning, the core of creative expression and the heart of self-management. Most wonderful of all, curiosity is the bringer of pleasure.

WE NEED CURIOSITY IN OUR digital and fast changing world more than ever. It keeps us agile and able to adapt to the constant changes within organisations. But what is curiosity? Where does it come from and how does it develop? And above all, how can we harness it and inject more curiosity into our busy lives?

In this chapter, we learn how curiosity comes to life, how it allows us to learn intellectual humility and how the wise ancients used curiosity at home, work and play.

Your Curious Intelligence

Over the last three decades, research has revealed that curious individuals learn faster and with more ease. They build stronger relationships and are more in control of their emotions. On top of that, curious people are just more interesting! They have stories to tell and knowledge to share, and they're interested in others. Curious people ask poignant questions because they're keen to unearth the true you. That's why curious teams are well positioned to transform conflict into collaboration and challenges into opportunity.

In the same way, curious organisations are able to build cultures that foster creativity and innovation. Curious leaders embrace intellectual humility and understand the importance of acknowledging what they don't know. They're willing to search for answers across the span and breadth of their organisation.

The benefits of curiosity are abundant, but how does curiosity achieve all of this? Let's delve in and find out.

With curiosity, everything starts with an exploration. Perhaps it is a cognitive search, like a question. Why is the earth round? Where does the sun go? What is grass made of? Why can't I have another biscuit? Or perhaps it is a sensory 'what if...'? What if I touch this hedgehog or eat that red berry?

This is how a child learns not to touch a hot plate and sense the pleasure of giving and receiving a hug. As they grow older, they learn that bullying brings unpleasant feelings and that gratitude does the reverse. As adults, we remember that warm sand feels good between the toes and that laughter is contagious. The response to our curiosity is interpreted and stored deep in the brain so it becomes part of each individual's learning journey.

Maria's Story

Let's meet Maria, an anthropologist, writer and lifelong adventurer. As a young girl Maria became fascinated by the North Pole. She wanted to know everything about it. She started reading books on the people of the Arctic. At the age of 10 she discovered how to build an igloo and she longed to see the northern lights.

As a young woman, she began to research the changing lifestyles and customs of the Inuit people, and on her 18th birthday visited Tuktuyaktuk on the Canadian Arctic to see for herself how they bury their food in the natural refrigerator that is the permafrost. She loved the adventure of exploring new places and meeting new people. But she also experienced how the people struggled to keep their customs and traditions alive in a world that was changing beyond their control.

She did a degree in anthropology (much to her father's disappointment as he wanted her to follow in his footsteps and become a doctor) and became an expert on climate challenges for people living in polar regions.

An advocate and a warrior, Maria is passionate about making a difference. She sees opportunities to use technology not only to share her findings with the largest audience possible, but also to aid the polar communities and help them gain a level of autonomy over their future.

Today, Maria continues to give lectures and write books. She has faced many challenges in her life and has built resilience to help her rebound from setbacks.

She remains curious; curious about herself, curious about others and curious about the world in which she lives. It is the very experiencing of her curiosity that makes Maria who she is.

Your Motivating Brain

A primary function of curiosity is to encourage learning, not just for children, but for all of us throughout our lives. When you are curious your brain offers an inherent reward of a pleasurable sensation, a mini high that makes you feel good. Best of all, this feel-good high encourages you to be curious again and again, as your brain anticipates yet another reward.

Curiosity lies at the heart of the intrinsic and extrinsic motivator-reward system. It is a hunger (motivation) that is satisfied (reward) by learning, discovery, interpretation and knowledge. So, the very prospect of reward becomes a drive, like hunger. The biological reason for this is simple – it's the essence of your survival instinct and it starts almost the moment you are born.

The brain's complicated and sophisticated neural system has several functions, one of which is to drive the motivator-reward system. This is why children from the youngest age learn to make sense of the world through experimenting. They use all five senses to test and explore the world around them. They make sounds to trigger a response: a smile, a laugh or an echo. Through touch they learn what is safe and what is dangerous. They listen, mimic and respond to praise (and criticism). As they grow, children question everything and tie together the threads of experience and knowledge to create patterns of behaviour, language and wisdom. They do it because they have learned that their curiosity is rewarded with pleasure.

As an adult you probably no longer feel the need to touch and test everything, yet you continue to be curious. Igniting your curiosity sends you on the path to knowing, understanding and sensing. You do this in three different ways.

1. EXPLORATION

This is what's happening when Maria reads a book and watches videos on how to build an igloo. She knows it is made of ice, but she doesn't know how to construct it to make it safe and keep her warm. There is a gap in her knowledge. She recognises what she doesn't know, switches on the ignition of curiosity and engages the natural learning process which propels her exploration. As Marcelo Staricoff, a fellow researcher of curiosity and author of *The Joy of Not Knowing*, would put it, she falls into the delightful pit of the unknown. Here, she gleans so much pleasure that she makes discoveries, consolidates her learning. Step by curious step, Maria climbs out of the pit of the unknown as she learns and begins to understand how a perfect igloo is constructed.

We all fall into our own pits of unknown many times. The unknown might be around a subject or about a particular issue. Or it may be more focused, researching into an area, learning how to do something specific or reading different points of view on a subject.

What are you learning about right now? Is it something that will bring you understanding and knowledge on a subject you want to know more about? This is your curiosity at work. It gains information, builds understanding and expands your repertoire of knowledge, not only making you more interested but more interesting too.

2. UNDERSTANDING

All of our thoughts are built on a series of perceptions – individual interpretations to help us understand the world around us. Your brain, a magnificent and powerful self-organising system, exists to simplify the complex world in which you live and to give your life context that is easy to understand and manage. But when a new phenomenon comes along, perhaps a concept that you have not come across before, (or a feeling, a sensation, a sound or a thought), you are forced to match your understanding of this new phenomenon with your existing paradigms. We all do this all the time. We create boxes or models of understanding and these become our paradigms. But then we face a new situation and have to match the new reality with our existing paradigm.

I have always loved water sport of any type. Just being on the water makes me happy. One day, while on a kayaking expedition off the Isle of Skye, our group got caught in an almighty storm and I had to use every ounce of my energy to paddle across a large expanse of open water to reach the safety of land. I felt an adrenaline rush that I wouldn't want to feel too often. It was a genuine sense of fear. I still love water sport of all types. But my understanding of sport that relies on nature has changed. I now have a deep respect for the potential dangers of water and this has harnessed my approach to risk in a good way.

So, curiosity also leads you to have an ever-deeper sense of understanding of the world. But this also forces you to match the outside world with your existing boxes and paradigms. And this often forces you to resolve the inconsistency between what it is that you're currently experiencing with what it is you already know. This is what happens when Maria tries to make sense of how her own lifestyle impacts on the lives of people many miles away. Until her journey to meet the people of the Arctic, she had never matched her shopping habits with the impact that consumer behaviour has on the climate.

Curiosity is powerful, but it can also bring temporary discomfort while we match our new learning with our existing ideas.

With this type of curiosity, you look for meaning and this allows you to align the old and new perception so you can adjust to a new reality. You balance the incongruity through learning. This is a crucial form of curiosity in light of the future of work and how it relates to our growing dependence on digital technology and our understanding of social change.

Perhaps you, like me, experience this juxtaposition through the uncomfortable tension between your need for autonomy and privacy, and your desire for an easy online experience. Did you hesitate when you considered downloading a Covid-19 tracing app? Maybe you find it hard to reconcile the way big data and algorithms streamline your internet searches while also converting your every action into a statistic. Perhaps, like me, you question your consumption of meat or the amount of waste you produce or the long-term impact of your short-term buying decisions.

Curiosity becomes key to a non-judgemental, honest appraisal of each of our choices in life. It's a responsibility and can steer us towards a purpose-led, rich and fulfilling future.

3. SENSING

The last of the three curious pathways is sensing, which allows us to experience what's around us through taste, touch, sound, smell, and sight.

- Tasting blue cheese, raspberries straight off the plant, or dark chocolate.
- Touching wet grass, a hot hob, broken glass.
- The smell of baking bread or a rose garden newly in bloom.
- Feeling the tickling of tadpoles on the palm of your hands.
- Hearing the chiming of church bells.
- Seeing the first blooms of spring.

In this curious pursuit you learn what brings pleasure and what brings pain, what to approach and what to avoid.

Babies and children use their senses to understand the world on a fundamental level. As an adult you do this to search for what makes you content or brings you peace of mind – or what brings sensations of anxiety or despair. Maria sees the Northern Lights and feels a great internal joy. From that first viewing she is drawn to step outside each night in search of not just the sight of the shimmering lights but the sensation of pleasure that it brings her. It is a cyclical process. It starts with an anticipation of pleasure sparked by a desire. This brings joy, which translates into a new anticipation of pleasure, which feeds into a circular motion of anticipation and reward.

We all nurture our curiosity in different ways; by reading novels, experiencing nature, through the sound of a full orchestra or the silence of church, in moulding clay or writing poetry. While there are certainly commonalities between people, our paths and interests are vastly different. When you do whatever you do, your clever mind determines which of those experiences brings pleasure and which don't. Without you noticing, your brain works hard to store this information deep in your subconscious. If a wet walk atop a windy ridge brought you delight, you'll be internally instructed to do it again and again. If you felt enormous excitement or compassion while reading a great book, you will no doubt feel the urge to pop down to your local book shop to hunt for its sequel.

What experiences bring you a great sense of joy? What makes you smile from the centre of your stomach? Is it reading a book, running in the rain, going to a concert, having a coffee with a friend, meeting someone new, going ice-skating or searching for bluebells in spring?

As you think about this, don't get side-tracked by once-in-a-lifetime experiences as those are difficult to replicate. Instead, concentrate on the small but powerful pleasures that can be repeated. When did you last do those things? Was it a long time ago? If so, why? What can you do to allow this to happen more often?

The motivator-reward system is a vital component of growth and development. It prompts learning and reflection. It arouses passions and interests. It cultivates mental well-being. However, after childhood it comes under regular battering from daily pressures, for some more than others. So, if we want more curiosity in our lives, we need to actively make space for it as we get older.

CULTIVATING CURIOSITY

SKILLS, ATTITUDES & BEHAVIOURS

DESCRIPTION

	DESCRIPTION
QUESTIONING	Promotes a culture of inquiry, not defense, allowing for positive change
HUMILITY	Knowing that you don't know something leads to new knowledge and wisdom
LEARNING	Creates the habit of life-long learning, supporting agility and resilience
EMPATHY	Feeling and imagining other people's emotions boosts emotional intelligence
COMPASSION	Creates the desire to take action to improve the lives of others
DIVERSITY	Promotes collaboration across sector/ skillset towards a common goal

Making Space for Curiosity

Curiosity is a hungry beast and responds well to constant feeding. Though binge-feeding is not ideal as the pleasure is more regular with frequent small portions. By not feeding curiosity at all, or only on occasion, the brain slowly learns not to bother searching for any remuneration. Your neural system releases less dopamine, you feel fewer small pleasures, and you experience even less curiosity. Over time this becomes your new norm.

Many people believe that the pressures of time, children, work and mortgages deprive them of small pleasures, but the challenge is to find opportunities for pleasure rather than simply presenting problems.

Vikram's Story

Let's meet another character, Vikram. When he was four, Vikram's parents moved from Rajasthan in Northern India to the UK so they could be closer to their extended family. Vikram is now a nurse at a large NHS hospital and is married to Mishka. They have two young children. Vikram commutes to work. It's an hour and 10 minutes each way, so he leaves early in the morning and often returns home after the children have gone to bed.

But not on Wednesdays. On Wednesday evenings he plays in a band – with Mishka and the children. They assemble their instruments, two guitars, a fiddle, and a plastic recorder and play together in the extension that they're slowly converting into an extended living space. For two hours they toot, hoot, scrape and laugh. It always takes a bit of excruciating pleading to prize the children away from their tablets and phones, but once the 'music' begins, they all have a great time.

At work, one crisis follows another, and on most days, Vikram is on his feet for the duration. Targets and financial constraints mean he has limited time with his patients. He rushes from bed to bed, inputting statistics and data on his work tablet as he goes. He loves his job, but experience has taught him the importance of taking time whenever possible to recharge his batteries. He does this by going on what he calls micro-hikes through the small hospital garden. He observes the plants, breathes in the scent of the cut grass, and lets his mind wander. On tough days he falls sleeps while listening to a podcast on his journey home.

Vikram takes care to feed his curiosity even when he's pushed to the limit. He creates family time through musical expression and he recognises the positive effect that quiet observation has on his physical and mental wellbeing.

We all have excuses for not being as curious as we could or want to be, but these are predominantly self-constructed obstacles. Although, if we construct these barriers, it means we can deconstruct them too. You can discover your own excuses through a two-step process of recognition and removal.

A simple way to become aware of your barriers is to first list them and then reflect on them, one at a time. Ask yourself: is this barrier imposed on me or is it self-imposed? Odds are that the majority are self-imposed and if that's the case, you can look to make small changes that allow you to take charge of the obstacle, rather than allowing it to take charge of you.

Remember, regular small portions of curiosity mean you get corresponding regular small portions of joy. So, doing the recognition and removal exercise is an important exercise for bringing curiosity back into your organisation. You might only be making tiny changes at a time, but lots of small steps can take you a long way.

Businesses that make space for curiosity nurture an organisation that's fertile with innovative thinking. Where individuals are encouraged to explore and spend time in the pit of the unknown, they become eager to share their knowledge, exchange ideas and collaborate across areas of expertise. This creates an organisation that's fun to work in and that leads individuals to strive for excellence.

By the same token, organisations that value productivity and exploitation over exploration run the risk of sucking the territory dry of creative seedlings and end up building a culture where team members seek to exist rather than thrive. These organisations consider curiosity superfluous, time wasting and extravagant and work hard to ensure that all working hours are spent solely in the pursuit of productivity. But as we have seen, this is a short-sighted strategy because gifted employees, now more than ever, value work they consider purposeful, meaningful, creative, collaborative and fun, and are willing to jump ship to find it.

Feeding Curiosity not Algorithms

In the twentieth century, high-speed travel and the internet added momentum to our lives; in the twenty-first century, it adds haste. The new trend often triggers a hunger for instant gratification fed in part by fast fashion, fast food and organisations such as Uber, Netflix and Amazon. The communication channels of social media and email demand our immediate attention and rapid response. For decades, we've wanted to get everything as quickly as possible. Today we want things *now.*

But there are dangers for us all here. By repeatedly appeasing our desire for instant gratification we affect the way the brain responds to the anticipation of reward. Over time, we've left ever-diminishing space between the urge to have and the response of getting. Curiosity doesn't have time to analyse whether what we want is a real desire that will bring long term pleasure or a temporary craving.

Let's unpick this a bit.

Imagine you're trying to choose between the newest, top-of-the-range tennis rackets online. You feel excited and decide to order one that promises excellent performance and looks really cool. One click. It feels great. It arrives the next morning and now you're really keen to give it a go, so you call John for a game in the afternoon. You're very pleased with your purchase and looking forward to trying it out on court. You and John play for an hour, but it's not quite the game you expected and the racket doesn't feel as amazing as you expected. John thinks the racket looks great and you're confident you'll play better now you have your new super-duper racket.

Perhaps the most forceful of the rushes in this short episode was the one immediately following the one click. Short but powerful, it gives you a rush of initial gratification as your curiosity anticipates a small amount of pleasure. Each time you give in to the short-term rush you strengthen the same neural pathway, building a habit that craves that exact sensation again and again.

In your quest for that moment of instant pleasure, more dopamine is released into your system so the very sight of your phone can induce a craving to shop. Curiosity and cravings both ignite the motivation-reward centre and the short-term effect of a rush of pleasure has a long-term effect that's detrimental to many aspects of your life – including your bank balance, your body and your mind.

Do you habitually check your emails, even though you know there is nothing urgent to respond to? This is the anticipation of the short-term rush of dopamine doing its stuff, egging you on in search of pleasure. Clever system. But what if you were able to exchange those short-term cravings for more moments of curiosity and equal amounts of pleasure?

The dependence on instant information can both ignite and dampen curiosity. How easy is it to fall down an internet-search rabbit hole and discover fascinating facts about something that 10 minutes ago you were not interested in? We have a world of information at the tips of our fingers. But for all that, the ease of finding that information can diminish the desire to explore. While Google, Baidu and other search engines offer an astonishing wealth of knowledge at the push of a button, the point is not always to get an immediate answer. Some occasions deserve a slower approach, an approach that savours the learning journey where exploration and discussion, the exchange of experiences and knowledge are the very point.

The next time you feel the urge to look up an answer on the internet, first simply reflect on the question. It only takes a few minutes to activate the curious neural pathways – and who knows where they will take you. One thing is for sure, your curiosity will take a different route to the well-carved paths that the machine learning algorithms would guide you down. And it would be your path, not the path of a large organisation driving you to an end that suits their needs rather than your own.

Data collection and analysis has the potential to endorse conformity as the digital algorithms behind search engines and social media drive us all down paths of allegiance. This is known as an echo chamber, a process in which your social feeds get narrower and narrower until all information coming your way coincides with your existing view. As a result, your beliefs are amplified and reinforced rather than questioned or challenged. That vital gap between what you know and what you learn is never opened so your curiosity is never sparked.

With the echo chamber, there is a danger that the absence of curiosity means it's easy to become even more immersed in extreme viewpoints, simply because you're encouraged to think what you've always thought through the support of your like-minded virtual community. It's easier to belong than to challenge. Even more frightening is that we disappear into echo chambers without even noticing, unknowingly triggering algorithms that curate our feeds.

This is how polarisation begins, and the results are huge and volatile camps of 'them' and 'us'. While social media hands us a huge treasure trove of information and entertainment, it also manipulates virtual communities in a way that can have disastrous consequences. History, ancient and modern, tells us that taking curiosity out of the equation can have very real and dangerous significance for many.

Social categorisation of 'them' and 'us' can also be detrimental to team and organisational performance. On a team level, if we strive too hard to conform to the majority, we are in danger of running headlong into groupthink with potentially disastrous results. On an organisational level it's easy to get caught in the trap of thinking from limited angles. For example, concentrating solely on data or competitor analysis rather than thinking creatively about future-focused strategic planning.

Curiosity: The Foundation of Liberty and Responsibility

As individuals we are all, to some extent, guilty of complacency – taking actions and behaving in ways that are void of curiosity. I've bought more than one cheap black T-shirt in the past 12 months without being curious as to its provenance. I didn't consider, for example, how much water was used to make it, where the cotton was grown or the conditions of the factory where it was assembled. I wasn't curious about the carbon footprint of its journey from factory to shelf, the journey from rubbish bin to waste disposal site or of the 120 years of slow decomposition of the fabric. But now that I've become curious, I've started to ask questions, and this is what I discovered.

The Aral Sea, formerly the fourth largest lake in the world with an area of some 68,000 km2 and once home to many thriving fishing communities, is now almost completely dry and is now considered an example of ecosystem collapse. It was mostly brought about by the building of irrigation channels. These were used to water the crops of fruit and vegetables needed for a burgeoning population. But crucially, these irrigation channels were also needed to quench the vast thirst of the cotton fields that supplied the demand for cheap cotton products.

In the short space of just 30 years, the Aral Sea has almost entirely disappeared and my purchase of that cheap black T-shirt plays a part in this story. My curiosity now makes me unable to shirk my responsibility for contributing to the loss of the sea. But now that I know, I can't become unaware of my findings. All I can do is choose either to be complacent or to change my behaviour. Liberty and responsibility have been exposed by curiosity.

Viktor Frankl proposes in his book *Man's Search for Meaning* that if the East Coast of the United States holds the Statue of Liberty, the West Coast should surely contain the Statue of Responsibility. If we are to ask for liberty, we must be ready to take responsibility. If we want civil rights, we must have civil responsibility too.

But many western countries have, over time, somehow created a culture where individual autonomy is given away in return for the right to lay blame for all troubles and woes on someone sitting somewhere in a position of power. As a society we want liberty, though only if it comes with limited responsibility. But if we as members of society don't take responsibility for the problems in our world then we can't claim the power to solve them either. Perhaps we can relieve a burden of responsibility by offloading them onto governments, but by doing so we tighten the shackles on our own freedom.

But where does this responsibility (or lack of it) stem from? The answer has to be curiosity – or the lack of it and our avoidance of questioning an issue or taking the trouble to research into the reasons behind it. This is why it's often easier to be complacent with our curiosity than delve into reasoning. This complacency does not necessarily stem from a general lack of care, but it is intricately linked to the present. It allows us to focus only on what is needed, desired or happening *now* without a proper analysis of the past or any deep respect for the future.

Curiosity is a powerful disposition. It has the capability to influence major and minor change. And we all have personal responsibility to bring about those changes. Perhaps there's something you do that would benefit from a soaking of curiosity – something small, that could be part of something big, something valuable, something that gives you autonomy over your part in the world.

The future of work is an increasingly complex puzzle due in part to the interconnectedness of everything. A burgeoning number of organisations now report organisational success based on a rigorous assessment of their company's impact on its workers, customers, community, and environment. They take into account their environment and social impact. They assess how well they look after their employees and the people in their wider area of influence. They rate their contribution to society and community. Some amend their legal governing documents to require their board of directors to balance profit and purpose. This is not just doing good. This is doing well by doing good. And it stems from a deep curiosity into the nature and impact of the organisation on the individual, the community and the world as a whole. From this, it's possible to see that curiosity is driving an organisational movement that is successful for all in many ways.

This is purposeful business, or ethically driven business. And many believe, as I do, that this is the way of the future. Young people, while they do value business and its role in larger society, place high value on purpose over profit. Indeed, numerous studies' report that millennials believe businesses in general are more ethical and society-focused than in 2015. But there is still a long way to go before the vision, mission and values of businesses can balance the emphasis on profit. And a lot of work to do before business expansion can be aligned with improvements in job satisfaction, skills training and customer experience.

That doesn't mean Millennials are not anti-profit, not at all. They see business as having a responsibility to make money. However, they place importance on a longer-term strategy rather than short-term maximization of profits. For Millennials, the strategy must be purpose-driven. According to a 2018 Edelman Earned Brand study 'nearly two-thirds (64 percent) of consumers around the world will buy or boycott a brand solely because of its position on a social or political issue.' It goes on to say that '53 percent believe that brands can do more to solve social ills than the government.' Now if you take into account that a large percentage of Millennials and Generation Z will only work for purpose-driven organisations, and that these very people, the Change Generation, will make up the majority of the workforce by 2025, you can see how the future of work needs to look very different to the way it does now.

Building Your Future based on a Curious Disposition

The Zen branch of Buddhism focuses on meditation and mindfulness. One of the core philosophies is the importance of gaining insight into the nature of things as they are, without intellectual reasoning. Travelling slowly over the ancient Silk Roads of Central Asia, Zen Buddhism originated in India. It passed through China and crossed the sea to Japan in the thirteenth century and then went by air to the West in the nineteenth century. The ancient message is as valuable today as it was then: release judgement, drop expectations and look at the world around you with new eyes – namely, those of a beginner.

Seeing things as if for the first time rejuvenates the sense of wonder and prevents you from taking things for granted. This has two large positive outcomes. Firstly, the rejuvenation of wonder creates positive emotions which builds your resilience artily. This is the broaden-and-build theory at play where positive emotions help you rebound more easily from stressful situations and help you find positive meaning in negative encounters. Being curious without judgement and being open to new ideas leads to an internal armoury of optimism and hopefulness. This becomes resilience. And resilient people perceive hindrances as opportunities and failures as successes.

Ironically, it takes practice to become a beginner! The best way to develop this habit is to keep practicing. In the early stages of training it can be tough to keep judgement at bay. But with practice you should be able to create space between the stimulus and response to park judgement, apply a beginner's mind and be curious.

Additionally, by parking your expert head and introducing a novice mentality you ignite the creative thought process. Without preconceptions there can be no pre-determined outcome. Without an assumption of what might occur, you simply apply curiosity and inquire where something could lead you. With an attitude of not knowing, you're much more likely to be open to new possibilities. As we have seen it can help to build your resilience armoury, but it's also a powerful tool to use any time you consider yourself to be the font of knowledge. In this situation judgement trumps curiosity and it's easy to fall into a downward spiral of negativity and stagnant thinking.

What, in your life at present, would benefit from you using a beginner's mind? Could it be that not having the answer is the key to your next breakthrough?

In organisations, experts often find it difficult to think creatively, to innovate, to look at problems from different angles or to change perspective. Beginners have no choice. Experts are hindered by know-how and familiarity and often become judgemental and stuck. Beginners explore and interrogate and look with fresh eyes. Imagine what could happen if you could apply a beginner's mind to your team and organisational setting.

One approach is to become the beginner yourself. This can require effort and determination. You need to favour questioning over answering, inquiry over experience. You need to remove judgement and set your mind free of hard trodden paths of experience. But note that the beginner's mind is a tool and as such it should be used appropriately. If injections of past experience can help the process, then you need to be able to move fluidly between expert and beginner.

How can you apply the beginner's mind? Practice makes perfect. Think of something that you would like to get a fresh perspective on. Perhaps a problem that has been bothering you, or a product or idea that you would like to think about creatively. Maybe there are tensions at work and you find yourself at loggerheads with a colleague or perhaps there is an ongoing issue with a faulty process. What if you knew nothing about this subject, what questions would you ask to gain an understanding of it? Don't cheat, it won't get you anywhere, you absolutely have to park all judgement and previous knowledge of this subject and really apply a beginner's mind.

To give you a simple example, a few months ago I found myself fuming with anger because Donald Trump expressed his desire to buy Greenland for the USA. Comments such as 'it is essentially a real estate deal' just helped to fuel the fire within me. Then I thought, stop, let me approach this with a beginner's mind. What if I knew nothing about Trump? What if I knew nothing about Greenland? What if I could remove all judgement and approach the issue leaving all pre-existing paradigms behind?

This led me to ask a few questions. Has any president tried to buy land before? And of course, the answer is yes, many times over. Alaska was purchased by the United States from Russia in 1867, Louisiana from France in 1803, Florida from Spain in 1819. This in turn led me to ponder on Hong Kong, which the Qing dynasty of China ceded to Great Britain in 1842, rather dubiously ending the first of the two Opium Wars. Which led me to think on today's matters of Cold War re-enactment between China and the West.

All of this thinking took roughly five minutes. The outcome? Well, I don't like Donald Trump any more than I did before, but by putting his real estate desire in a 'new' context I was able to remove the emotion and judgement and reflect on the situation in a more global context.

To integrate the beginner's mind into your organisation, deliberately invite people who are not experts on a subject or issue to meetings. Include them in discussions. Ask them questions and listen to what they say with the intention of understanding their point of view. Value the cross fertilisation and the exchange of ideas and perspectives. Inject the beginner's mind into meetings, brainstorming sessions, strategy sessions and even tea breaks. Build a community that feeds on the energy of sharing. In doing so, you'll naturally build on both the breadth and the depth of your shared knowledge as a team. And it's in this space that ideas crash and combine, fizzle and bubble, and where the real potential of creativity and innovation lies.

Curiosity and Lifelong Learning

Remember Maria? She created a long-term development path that mutated over her career. She moved from physical exploration and teaching to lecturing and then to writing books and articles. Now, in her later life, she continues to earn a living and stay engaged with her subject and with the world around her. She feels great that she can still contribute and add value, but at her own speed.

From the outset of your journey towards greater knowing, understanding and making sense of the world around you, it's curiosity that leads you along the fascinating path of wisdom. The trail winds around barriers, climbs challenges and rollercoasters down gullies of excitement. Via the motivator-reward system it brings you alive, alerting all your senses to the small wonders and miracles around you. Your curiosity offers you amity and affection through developing empathy and building relationships, and with that comes recognition and acceptance. It ignites appreciation, consciousness and compassion. And it promises adventure and marvel.

If you chose to take time to nurture and feed your curiosity, to give it time and space, it will reward you with endless pleasures.

Chapter 3

_____

Creativity

Everyone has creative potential, you just need to know how to access it. There are different tools and techniques to use to help you access yours. Understanding where creativity comes from is the first step to being able to tap into it, so you can use it in a range of different scenarios.

DESPITE TEACHING CREATIVE THINKING IN many organisations and universities for many years, our masterclasses still start with the same question: 'Who here is creative?'

What's interesting is the fact that we get almost the same response every time. Around 2% tentatively raise their hand, suggesting they have a personal belief that they're creative but are wary of admitting it. But the shocking reality is that less than 10% of people in higher education or employment think they're creative.

And yet, if you ask a bunch of school children under the age of 13 the same question, the answer is staggeringly different – more than 80% believe they're creative. That can only mean something goes horribly wrong between the ages of 12 and 19 in terms of the way we perceive our own levels of creativity.

Perceptions of Creativity

We are all born creative, but we spend many years of our life learning not to be. It's not that the skill goes away, it doesn't. We just lose the will to use our creativity because we think we don't need it. As a result, our creativity atrophies as we race to grow and get more productive.

As automation speeds up processes, so results speed up too and suddenly everything appears to be moving really quickly. When that happens, it's easy to feel we all have to do more – and do it faster. But how can you find the time to be creative when you're programmed to be productive and spend all your time, energy and effort searching for increased productivity. All this to the detriment of your creativity, which means before long, creativity becomes a forgotten skill and you lose confidence in your creative potential.

Here are just a few signs that you're more creative than you think:

- You've opened your kitchen cabinets to find a strange combination of ingredients that you've proceeded to combine into a delicious new dish.
- If you're a parent and you've invented games with your kids.

- You've recently solved a problem (large or small) and been pretty pleased about the results.

Can you think of any other situations where you've improvised or made things up? If so, it's proof that you're creative.

The truth is that creativity is a thought process and that means it can be trained, like a muscle, so with patience, confidence and determination it can developed to get stronger. If you want to build your creative muscle, you simply need to stimulate new neural connections and you can do that by expanding the range of thoughts and ideas you expose yourself to.

In other words, you need to feed your brain and flex your thinking muscles. The easiest way to do this is to question, link, observe, associate and network. But to do that, you need to experiment and be curious.

Like all muscles, your brain needs time to recover too. Creative recovery includes sleep, daydreaming, playing and relaxing. You must allow time for this because your mind needs it. Your brain needs space so it can sort, clear, organise, store and prepare itself for yet more stimulation.

Fortunately, this is a natural process, because our brains are self-organising systems of epic proportion. Their job is to make our world simple so we can achieve the mundane and the complicated. They are at work 24 hours a day, either in Task Mode – thinking, analysing, doing, achieving, or in Default Mode – sorting, clearing, organising and storing information. The Task Mode helps us get things done; the Default Mode helps us to simply be. Both are vital for creative thinking, living and being.

Be honest with yourself. How much time do you spend being busy with busyness, searching for higher levels of personal efficacy? And how much time do you spend being creative? Are the two in balance?

As your neural tendrils spread and search to form new pathways, they crash and collide and stimulate new thoughts and ideas. This is what happens when you begin to rebuild your creative muscle. And as an added bonus that wonderful motivator-reward system of curiosity releases dopamine which makes you feel great, so you want to do more. This is how creative thinking feeds yet more creative thinking. As your muscles get stronger, your desire to think creatively gets stronger too.

Components of Creativity

To develop your creativity, you need to encourage the development of three key approaches in your life:

1. Adventure, which brings a sense of play and experimentation.
2. Mastery, which is the determined practice of a particular skill.
3. Insight or the ability to reflect on how well you're doing.

Above all, you need to be confident of who you are as an individual and have the capacity to enjoy the differences between you and others.

Creativity is more than having an idea. It is about having an idea that can be turned into something beautiful, or useful, or preferably both. So, being creative isn't just about generating ideas; it's about transforming those ideas into something real. This is how creative thought turns into something of value. An idea for a new product is not enough in itself, it needs to be followed up in an iterative cycle of research, building, and testing in order to be of use. Likewise, an idea for an improved procedural method has no value unless it's acted on and applied.

Creative thinking comprises an overlapping partnership of expertise, attitudes and behaviours, and thinking skills. To develop high levels of creativity you need to focus your efforts on developing all three of these areas, so let's take a look at what they entail.

1.   EXPERTISE

Expertise is your subject speciality. This might encompass your profession – perhaps you are a mathematician or a musician, a lawyer or plumber. It might encompass your area of expertise – geography teacher or human rights lawyer. Or it might encompass a combination of areas in the same way that Sir David Attenborough is a superb and experienced TV presenter and an expert in many aspects of the natural world.

To develop your creativity, you need to expand your expertise on two levels: breadth and depth. A paradigm that helps us understand this is the T Model where breadth of knowledge is depicted as the horizontal top line and depth of knowledge the vertical line. By developing your proficiency in line with the T Model, you encourage the expansion of your subject-specific expertise at the same time as developing complementary broad and transferable skills, which make it easier for you to adapt what you know in any situation.

T Model of Learning and Being

Breadth of Knowledge
Adventure, explore, experiment, maximise variety

Depth of Experience
Practice, reflect, analyse, master

Combine

While depth delivers mastery in your specific subject area, breadth allows you to cross boundaries with competences such as collaboration, empathy and good communication skills. The interdisciplinary nature of the model sets you up for long-lasting success because you have the ability to adapt and change, and to apply your skills and knowledge in different scenarios. According to Tim Brown of IDEO, it is deep knowledge (the vertical stroke of the T) that allows individuals to contribute their expertise to the creative process. By contrast, the curious quality of the horizontal stroke allows for cross-discipline collaboration, another crucial part of the creative process.

If you are already developing the breadth and depth of

your 'T' then you are in good stead. But for your working future, perhaps you could think beyond the 'T' to the 'Key'. The 'Key' is a model that reveals how additional areas of expertise add disciplinary agility to your portfolio.

Key Model of Learning and Being

The key represents your unique variety of knowledge and expertise, and like a key used in a lock, can open doors to insights and new solutions. As you can see in the diagram above, the key has several notches down the length of its central spine. The notches are different sizes, representing the varying level of knowledge in particular subject areas. Some are short because they're in their infancy stage, indicating that you've taken up a new interest or developed a new skill. Others are deeper and more pronounced, indicating you have more expertise or knowledge in these areas.

What's so useful about developing more teeth in your key is that you are building yet more opportunities for the cross fertilisation of ideas. It helps you develop into what Elon Musk calls an 'expert-generalist'. You also lengthen the spine of your key as you cover more subject areas, and by doing so, you broaden your cross disciplinary skills. This is how you add to both your mastery of different areas of expertise and your interpersonal skill set, which together act to build your creative capacity.

Clara's Story

Clara started working in the fashion industry straight after she left university. She specialised in high-end street fashion and discovered a passion for the design of swim and gym wear. By specialising, the spine of her key grew thicker while her key's teeth develop as she broadened her range of expertise.

Over the years she became aware of the challenges of the fashion industry and saw the impact that fast fashion has on the environment, and on society. She began to research circular economy, remanufacturing and ethical supply chain management, adding yet more substantial teeth to her every thickening key.

At the age of 32, Clara stepped away from fast, high-end fashion and started her own sustainable swim and gym wear company. Her supply chain is made up entirely of women, starting with small NGOs in the Pacific and ending with local craftswomen in her hometown. Her material is ... discarded fishing nets, which her organisation collects from the sea, remanufactures into long lasting material and cuts into stunning contemporary designs.

By developing both the spine and the teeth of her key, Clara was able to create a company that is driven by her passion for doing well in business and doing good in the world. Even more importantly, she loves it!

These questions will help you think about your own Key Model. Use any method you like to answer these questions: write, draw, rest, sing, paint... Use all your creativity to form an impression of your key.

- What does your key look like right now?
- How do you need to develop it so it gives you the creative edge?
- What interdisciplinary skills are you developing to broaden the spine of your key?
- What new areas of expertise are you pursuing to add new notches to your key?

2. ATTITUDES AND BEHAVIOURS

By now, you hopefully have a sense of your creative potential. You realise that you are in fact pretty darn creative and there is space for even more creativity in your life. You also understand that creativity isn't just for artists, painters, musicians or design gurus. Nor it is just for those working in the creative industries. You understand that opportunities for creativity exist in every procedure, every plan, every decision and every thought process.

While creative accounting sounds somewhat dubious, examples of real creativity in accounting abound and the results bring value to many. Businesses of all sizes are now able to complete their bookkeeping using an online banking system prior to sending the information to HMRC for tax filing – and all with just a few clicks. Of course, this process is more complicated for larger businesses, but the act of constant creativity in the field of accounting has found opportunities for combining different types of technology to make the process of bookkeeping, accounting and tax filing streamlined. So, as you can see, there is space for creativity in everything, including parenthood, research, design, marketing, teaching, cooking and of course, accounting. Which rather begs the question as to why so many people believe that they are not creative.

One important factor is lack of self-belief. Another is the years of focusing on productivity and efficiency over creative exploration. And then there are the creative barriers, the noisy distractions that hinder creative potential. When working with businesses to develop creativity in teams and organisations, we list out the common barriers to creativity. Do any of these resonate with you?

- Lack of time.
- Too much pressure.
- Fear of failure.
- Fear of being wrong.

All these barriers are real, but more interestingly, they're also self-imposed – at least to some extent. This is where attitude comes into the creativity equation. Creative individuals develop the breadth and depth of their skills and knowledge, but they also take ownership of their challenges. By doing this, they find the strength they need to build behaviours that untangle the web of self-imposed fears and pressures.

What can you do to allow for more creativity? What behaviours can you change? And what attitudes can you build that would facilitate the removal of some barriers and the injection of more creative thinking into your daily life?

3. THINKING SKILLS

With two of the interlocking elements of creativity under our belts, it's time to move on to the final element: creative thinking skills. These skills are all about applying different types of thinking to different situations. It's important to understand why creative thinking should be considered a skill, and discover what tools and techniques there are to help us think in a particular way that's suited to a particular situation.

Problems come in all shapes, sizes and levels of complexity. Each one requires a different level of attention and can benefit from a range of approaches. Creative problem solving and decision making includes selecting the most appropriate thinking style to suit the problem, for example:

- If you're getting stuck in your thinking and going around in circles, a lateral out-of-the-box thinking style would be a suitable option.
- If you you're being overly opinionated on any subject, you could perhaps benefit from some directed thinking as this will help you look at it from a different angle and see the problem anew.

- If you're having trouble coming up with fresh ideas, then you need some tools to stimulate idea generation.

Let's look at these in a bit more detail.

Directed thinking is purposeful, focused and timebound. It directs you to think from certain points of view at any one time, separating out your thinking and not allowing for any overlaps of opposing thoughts.

A simple tool to help you do this is to look at the problem from three different viewpoints. The thinking must be separated to be beneficial. Let's take the example of whether people should eat meat. Whichever side of the fence you stand on, you no doubt have a firm opinion on the matter. Your perspective is probably laced with a certain amount of judgement and self-righteousness, which is a natural reaction to any controversial issue.

Let's spend a couple of minutes looking at this issue from three different perspectives.

1. Spend 30 seconds considering the point of view that, 'Yes, people should eat meat'.
2. Next, spend 30 seconds coming up with as many reasons as possible why people should *not* eat meat.
3. To complete the exercise, take 30 seconds to think why people should maybe eat meat.

As you can see, this exercise in directed thinking separates out your thoughts, forcing you to come up with ideas that go against your personal judgement and offering space for new ideas.

Is there something that you are working on that would benefit from a short session of directed thinking? Try a quick 'yes', 'no', 'maybe' exercise to make space for some creative thought.

Lateral thinking is about stepping away from a problem and looking at it from an entirely different angle, i.e. from the side or above or even from underneath.

Lateral thinking takes a creative approach to a problem and using reasoning that is not immediately obvious or logical but that stimulates new ideas from unusual places. Again, let's use a simple example.

> Antonia arrives 20 minutes late to an important meeting with her senior colleagues. They are naturally annoyed, no more so than her direct boss, Lucas. He thinks her behaviour is rude, unprofessional and selfish, and now he is going to have to give Antonia's presentation without preparation.

Now let us try to apply some lateral thinking on this situation. Spend just one minute considering, without judgement, all the possible reasons why Antonia was late. Here are some ideas to get you started:

- She might have missed the bus or got stuck in unusually bad traffic.
- There might have been a problem when dropping off the children at school.
- Perhaps she got a flat tyre on the way to the office.
- Maybe she's doing it on purpose to annoy Lucas as retaliation for the comments he made yesterday.
- Perhaps she's terrified of public speaking but has never found the opportunity to tell her boss and she's been overcome with terror at the thought of having to give the presentation.

As you can see, there are many possible reasons why Antonia is late, but it's only by taking a minute to consider them all that you can change your perspective.

There are two big benefits to lateral thinking: the first is that it shifts your own emotional state. Lucas' first response was annoyance, but with more options he might feel calmer or at least slightly less annoyed, so allowing him think clearly and stay focused on the meeting.

The second benefit to lateral thinking is that it allows you to create a space to deal with the situation in a rational, rather than emotional way, heightening your emotional intelligence and your ability to deal with difficult situations.

Lateral thinking was a term first coined by Edward de Bono in the 1980s. As a tool, it can really help you to take a creative out-of-the-box approach to problem solving, an approach that can give you and your organisation a competitive advantage because you can find unique solutions to old problems.

Putting things together in new ways is at the core of creative thinking and a lateral approach makes it easier to find an alternative approach to a problem. As John Cleese so succinctly put it in his 2001 Ted Talk, 'Creativity is not a talent, but an operating system'. By questioning the status quo, or by searching to understand something new, we open our minds to new worlds and opportunities as well as new ways of thinking, seeing and being.

Creative Intelligence on a Team Level

Creative teams thrive on ambiguity and move effortlessly between divergent, spacious thinking and convergent, analytical thinking. They are able to use different thinking styles appropriately in order to generate alternatives and options before closing in and choosing the best solution.

Creative problem solving is a combination of divergent and convergent thinking. Divergent thinking makes it possible to look at an issue from different angles in order to put ideas, knowledge and solutions together in new combinations. Convergent thinking is the process of analysing the options available and choosing the best response.

Jasmine's story

Let's meet Jasmine. Jasmine is a partner in an Equity Firm managing investments for private individuals. It's a small organisation with 12 partners and 35 support staff.

Her responsibilities include:

- Improving internal systems.
- Client management.
- Managing her team.
- Business development.
- Finding new clients through networking and sales.

Over the three years she's been in her role, Jasmine has been purposefully fostering a culture of creativity in her team. She conducts monthly 'What if...?' sessions with them, so they can explore ideas and possible solutions to existing problems without judgement.

At each meeting, different team members bring problems they're working on to the table. At the start of the meeting, they vote on which issues they're going to focus on. They then spend two hours using different creative thinking techniques to come up with potential solutions to the issues they've selected.

These sessions have changed the way the team operates. As a result, they've introduced new procedures that facilitate greater productivity and spend more time on client management. In the last 18 months the company has seen a large increase in customer numbers and profitability due to the creative approach to problem solving used by Jasmine's team.

Jasmine has also spent time building a culture that supports risk taking. She's taught her team to see failure as a learning opportunity. Her team members are encouraged to share responsibilities and accountability to create a safety net that allows them to push beyond normal patterns of working, so they can freely test new ideas and solutions.

Successes and failures are both celebrated equally. Staff turnover is almost non-existent because each team member is motivated by their work and shares a sense of purpose with the rest of the team. They each feel valued and able to contribute to the company's success. The ability to think creatively develops confidence, stamina and determination in individuals and the teams that they are in. Creative individuals thrive in adversity, they reframe challenges into opportunities and look for solutions even when they're in the deepest of trenches. Of course, any approach must also be useful and actionable if it's going to be fit to be applied to a new product or a new process within the organisational context.

Creative thinking in line with Jasmine's approach can't be conducted in isolation; it requires organisational support in the form of a framework that fosters creativity and provides a safety net for failure. Part of that framework is an understanding that reflecting on failure offers opportunity for success. So, a truly creative organisation forms and shares clear goals and strategies, but then gives its employees the freedom and autonomy they need to move forward and deliver that goal in the best way possible.

Whatever your line of work, the challenges you face are broad in scope. There is a constant sense of urgency around coming up with creative solutions to a whole array of problems – social, financial and procedural. Your creative potential lies in your ability to combine previously unrelated ideas and see opportunities in a gnarly uncertain pool of challenges.

Succeeding within a landscape of technological transformation and tumultuous change depends on the development of both the breadth of your skills and the depth of your knowledge. You need broad skills that are easily transferable, making you agile and able to adapt. And you need a depth of knowledge in different areas, so you can act as a specialist, guru and expert when required. By building both breadth and depth you create a rich portfolio of skills, attitudes and knowledge that lays a firm foundation for creative thinking and problem solving.

The key significant benefit of developing creative muscle is that you build your confidence, which in turn allows you to build on your strengths, imagine a future, and persistently strive towards large and small achievements. Two added bonuses of creativity are that it leads to better social skills and higher levels of emotional intelligence, which in turn make for smoother and more harmonious working relationships, which, in turn, facilitate even greater levels of creativity.

Creative individuals know that cutting-edge new ideas are born from combining existing ideas then twisting and reconfiguring them to create ingenious new inventions. To do this, these individuals know they need to constantly seek collaborative opportunities and develop essential social skills to nurture partnerships and alliances. This leads us on to the next chapter where I talk about being connected: to self, to others and to the world in which we live. You have begun to build a more curious disposition and have also opened the door of your creative potential. But how do you use this new knowledge to work on yourself and collaborate with others to create things that are both beautiful and useful?

Chapter 4:

Connectedness

Humans connect in many ways – to ourselves, to others and to the world around us. As we continue on our own winding career paths, connectedness is perhaps the most vital of the human intelligences. We have a need to grow, to progress, to succeed, to feel fulfilled – this is an intrinsic part of the human condition.

OUR CONNECTEDNESS AS HUMANS STARTS with our connection to ourselves, which is why we all need to nurture ourselves to greater self-awareness, self-management and self-care.

The second level of connection is to others, via social gatherings as it helps to ensure authentic, congruent relationships with those around us.

The third connection we have is with the world in which we live; the landscape, the flora and fauna, global politics and attitudinal change as well as the holistic nature and interconnectedness of everything. Now, more than ever, it's important that we understand the long-term benefits of being connected to the world.

Connected to Self

The starting point for understanding ourselves is knowing what makes us tick, what we love, what we're good at and what we enjoy. We also need to know what our values and beliefs are and why.

Christina's Story

Graduating cum Lauda from her undergraduate degree, Christina has become an expert in marketing. A second-generation British Ghanaian, she has had to carve her own identity and it's not always been an easy ride. But she's been lucky in that opportunities have often presented themselves, and at times she has struggled to know which path to choose.

Charismatic and tenacious, Christina has always enjoyed the freedom that self-employment offers, but wonders if she would achieve more and make a bigger impact if she was working with a team that was out to make a difference. She is torn between her sense of autonomy and her need to contribute in a meaningful way.

When you get close to understanding yourself, you put yourself in a position where you can both create your own destiny, learn empathy and compassion for others, and develop the desire to improve the lives of others. This is the beating heart of building good relationships, leadership and team management.

Building intrinsic motivation

Back in the 1960s American psychiatrist Dr David McClelland conducted substantial research into what he called Psychological Needs. His findings resulted in a taxonomy of three major emotional needs that he believes all humans possess. Those needs are for:

1. Autonomy.
2. Achievement.
3. Affiliation.

McClelland's concept of autonomy describes the need for choice and the most important choice of all is the ability to choose what you do and how you do it. This sense of volition drives you to grow as an individual. If you remember back to the earlier chapter on curiosity, you'll remember that we're all born curious.

As a human being, you have a deep-rooted need to be able to choose what to pursue in your life, and this is directly linked with your intrinsic motivation. Your motivation comes from doing something that you're internally interested in and because of the inherent pleasure in doing the task. It's likely you feel empowered when you have a sense of choice and you're likely to feel good when you have control over how you approach and complete a task.

AUTONOMY

The first need McClelland identified is for autonomy. This is especially important at work. If you lead a team of people, notice whether you give your team members autonomy over how they decide to get their job done or whether you micro-manage and watch their every step. Happy teams are made up of individuals who are pursuing a common goal but getting there in their own way. Their mistakes and successes are owned and they build to create a constellation they can follow and which guides their next move.

ACHIEVEMENT

The second need is for achievement, which comes from a basic human drive to want to do well. This could be expressed as mastering a skill or passing a test. It might also take the form of becoming confident in public speaking or performing a concerto to a packed audience. Or it could be feeling confident at work and knowing you're gaining skills and knowledge that builds your expertise in your chosen subject area.

Achievement is an important psychological need, allowing you to be in control of your own outcomes and control your own mastery. Motivation, reward and ownership. This is emotional empowerment at its best.

AFFILIATION

The third and final need is for affiliation, the desire to connect to others. When I ask people to think of a time when they were really happy and feeling good, they always describe a moment shared with someone else, be it a family member, a loved one, a friend or a colleague. Happiness is closely linked to our sense of belonging.

Sitting at the core of our motivation and reward system, these three emotional needs get us out of bed in the morning and drive us to learn, grow and develop. They help us make difficult choices and undertake challenging tasks. In return, they offer great rewards. Rewards of belonging, of loving and being loved, of success, of purposeful power and control.

Each of us has all three psychological needs, but one's likely to be more dominant than the others. This becomes our main motivating force. Meeting this dominant need creates contentment and fulfilment. If it's thwarted, we suffer. Christina has a dominant need for autonomy; she cherishes the freedom that being her own boss affords. But she's also driven to make a difference and to achieve through her area of expertise.

Which is your dominant need? Look back over the past six months and look for evidence that this is your main psychological need. Think about your current role and consider whether you're meeting this need on a regular basis. Go a step further and think about each member of your team and consider whether you're aware of their dominant need. Are you managing them appropriately to tap into their sense of self-determination and intrinsic motivation? And if you have sense that you could be more individualised in your approach with your team members, how could you get to better understand their dominant need?

TOWARDS GREATER SELF-AWARENESS

A tool to help you on the path to knowing yourself is the Purpose Venn Diagram, assembled by Andrés Zuzunaga, a

Spanish astrologer and entrepreneur. It brings together two models; Ikigai and the Hedgehog model.

The Japanese concept of Ikigai focuses on your sense of purpose or your reason for being. Ikigai literally translates as: iki, meaning to live; and gai, meaning reason. Jim Collins' Hedgehog principle, from his best-selling book *Good to Great,* combines your sense of purpose with your ability to create a meaningful and prosperous career.

ZUZUNAGA VENN DIAGRAM

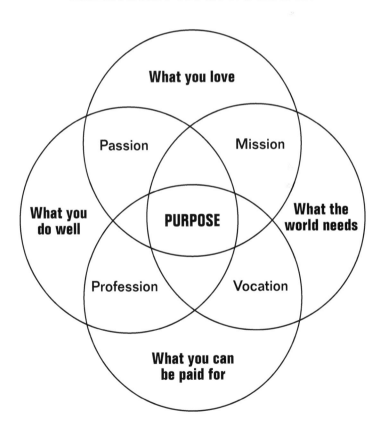

The Zuzunaga model is made up of four overlapping areas of your life that come together to offer an understanding of your mission, passion, profession and vocation. Let's take a closer look at each of the four areas to see if, by reflecting on them one by one, you can move a step closer to fully understanding your sense of purpose.

Passion: The combination of what you love to do and what you are good at is your passion. In this area your passion is ignited by the conjoining of energy from what you love and confidence from what you are good at. This is a powerful union.

Profession: The overlap between what you're good at and what you can be paid for is an indication of your profession. Your profession tends to be based on what you're skilled at and what you're trained to do.

Vocation: By contrast, your vocation is indicated by an overlap between what you can be paid for and what the world needs. Coming from the Latin 'vocare' to call, a vocation leans towards benefitting others and society as a whole, rather than just being a monetary quest. So your vocation has sense of a calling about it and is connected to your perception of what the world needs.

Mission: Your mission is defined by the overlap between what the world needs and what you love. Each and every one of us has our own perception of what the world needs. From talking to people on this subject, I've discovered that those who are proactively doing something about what they love report a higher level of personal well-being than those who are reactive and passive. We each have our personal battles to fight, be it environment, sustainability, caring for people, human rights, politics, society, animal welfare, etc. What you list in this area is more than a concern; it needs to be something you're willing to act on to change, even if you can only change it in a small way.

Purpose: Bang in the centre of all of these areas is your purpose, your raison d'être. The basic concept of Ikigai, or purpose, can be found in different philosophies from around the world, and perhaps the best known in the Western world is the logotherapy of Austrian psychiatrist and Auschwitz survivor, Victor Frankl. Frankl believed that we are all strongly motivated to live purposefully and meaningfully, and to do so must begin to understand our passion, mission, vocation and profession. If we can do this, Frankl claims, we can grow as individuals by acting meaningfully and responding purposefully to all of life's challenges.

Christina loves to use her voice and charisma to influence others. She took a leading role both in the #MeToo protests in 2018 and in the #BlackLivesMatter protests of 2020. She's good at marketing and gets paid well for her work. She chooses to use her expertise to make a difference in the world. She has a fairly vivid picture of her Ikigai.

Spend a little time thinking about your own Ikigai.

1. What you are good at?
2. What do you love?
3. What does the world need?
4. What can you be paid for?

When you've done that, consider these questions:

1. How well do you understand your mission, vocation, passion and profession?
2. What are you doing now that's in alignment with each of these areas?
3. Is there anything you could or should change based on your reflections?

Connected to Others

A sports massage therapist told me a story about a small but meaningful epiphany she had regarding the benefits of connecting with others. She's a busy woman and, like many of us, has started to make certain purchases online for ease and speed of delivery. In her case, she started buying rolls of massage bed hygiene paper online.

But one day she was curious about whether she would be able to source them locally and found a supplier just 1.5km from her home. She walked to the shop, getting 30 minutes of exercise and had a really great chat with the shop owner who, she discovered, supplies many other massage therapists in the area. She took a different route home, walking along the winding lanes, which were lined with local shops bustling with energy and life.

She felt vibrantly alive when she got home. She had supported a local business, learned about the state of her industry and competitors in her town, completed over an hour of exercise by walking there and back, and connected with her local area. She also increased her professional presence by becoming part of the local massage therapy community. Such were the benefits of connecting that she now buys paper massage bed rolls more often than she needs!

This story shows that, while it's possible to live life without being connected to others, we end up living a poorer life as a result. As human beings we're wired to connect to others. Social connection makes us feel good; it gives us a sense of identity and belonging. To quote the research professor at the University of Houston, Brené Brown, 'We are biologically, cognitively, physically, and spiritually wired to love, be loved, and to belong.'

The benefits of nurturing strong bonds in our communities include resilience, high self-esteem, positivity and a high level of emotional intelligence. Strong social connections are also proven to reduce anxiety and depression, and increase physical and psychological health.

But it's important to remember that social connection has little to do with the number of friends you have on Facebook or followers on LinkedIn. Social connection is about being emotionally connected to others on a level that allows for friendship and bonding. It's about building social capital that serves the purpose of protecting us when times get tough – and it's about sharing celebrations when times are good. Those who've built strong social networks are more likely to be resilient in times of trouble. They have people around them to talk with, to go to for support and to celebrate with.

Virtual Communication

Digital technology has changed the way we all communicate, and the three-month lockdown in the early stages of the coronavirus pandemic gave us all ample opportunity to discover the highs and lows of virtual communication! What would we have done without it?

At work, the synchronous communication channels of Zoom and Skype as well as asynchronous email, text and chat allowed for sophisticated levels of team interaction. But I heard many reports of miscommunication, misunderstanding, feelings of isolation and vulnerability from those working with clients during the lockdown. Asynchronous communication provides plenty of opportunity for trouble, be it in communication with your mother-in-law or your team members.

In face to face communication, the message being transmitted is made up of two aspects – verbal and non-verbal. Our non-verbal communication (facial expressions and body language) make up 55% of the messages we transmit. Think of Mr Bean – he can tell an entire story without saying a single word.

Vocal inflections constitute another 38% of the messages we conveyed, with only the final 7% of what we say coming from the words themselves. On top of this there is the process to take into consideration. Communication, by its very nature, is a two-way process that involves at least two people: the sender and the receiver.

Because there are so many connotations to every word, and even more implications in every sentence, the sender uses non-verbal methods to try to make the message as clear as possible. The receiver, if they are a good listener, might check for understanding by probing and reflecting or might use their body to respond, so creating a two-way feedback mechanism.

Digital communication can only simulate the real thing. By taking away the face to face aspect, the communication lacks the subconscious messages communicated via body language, intonation, facial expressions and gestures. It's stripped down to its bare essentials, a verbally based message void of any non-verbal connotations or emotional context.

This is why digital communication gives us only a fraction of the message. Of course, digital communication has its place and indeed its value. But without accompanying physical clues, there's a big risk of misunderstanding because it lacks the two-way non-verbal feedback mechanism of a face to face conversation.

Understanding the difference between digital and face to face communication is a vital part of mastering how you connect with others. Good communication is a strategic choice. A wise communicator understands what they're trying to achieve with each bit of their communication. They know how to adapt what they say to disseminate information or clarify it. They understand the different challenges of explaining and exploring an idea. They know what's needed to build trust and to bond.

Do you know your communication goals? For example, are you trying to reach out and expand your network or are you collaborating with others towards a shared goal? If you understand your intentions, you have a better chance of choosing the most appropriate channel for your message. And of course, nothing can beat the real face to face communication over a cup of tea.

Have you recently been in a situation when you've been talking to someone through a synchronous channel, such as a video conferencing system, when face to face would have been far more constructive? In future, is there a way that you can change a few small habits to ensure more face to face contact with people who are important to you at work and home?

Connected Intelligence in Organisations

Great business outcomes are built on the foundation of strong relationships. Your team and your people are the heart of your organisation. Technology has undoubtably increased productivity across all industries, but the real business risks and opportunities lie in the interfaces between people.

Relationships are more important than any amount of technology because, while the technology can automate and expedite processes, the real pace of business is reliant on the quality of personal interactions. Agile, fast-moving organisations are not successful when they use the words 'agility' and 'speed' as an excuse to increase productivity and profitability at the expense of employee burnout.

Successful agile and fast-moving organisations appreciate the benefits of relationships across the board – vertical, horizontal, internal and external. Real growth comes from the cross fertilisation, the spreading and diffusing of ideas and the nurturing of the organisation's bridge connectors: the human synthesisers. It is the connection between silos that makes creativity work. Human behaviour drives the success that all organisations crave. As the leader of a team or business, you need to know how to tap into the heart of human psychology to foster a team identity focused on success. The human dimension is everything.

Purpose-driven organisations are without a doubt the future of work. In successful organisations, values and purpose have moved beyond branded messages and drive the company's actions and behaviours. But there are still organisations that have yet to make the shift into the future. An organisation without a clear human-centred purpose has the tendency to withhold key information about the direction the company's going in, only sharing it with the senior team, who direct the workforce through micro-management.

The problem with this approach is that it's often demoralising to employees. It's also inefficient and dehumanising, which only results in high levels of disengagement among team members. An organisation with a clear human-centred purpose can engage the workforce through transparency and excellent communication, so they believe in the vision and actively engage with it. This connected approach is empowering, energising and collaborative resulting in moti-vated and engaged teams finding their own ways to steer toward organisational success.

One major aspect of building connectedness with others is putting a proper value on diversity in teams. Many organi-sations give lip service to diversity with framed posters on the office walls advocating its importance in the workplace. But few organisations make explicit the intrinsic value of team diver-sity. Nor do they spend time or energy building a framework that encourages a united team of people from different back-grounds, different ages and different thinking preferences.

Diversity has many forms. In terms of transparency, surface level diversity, such as age, gender and race can be easily seen. These surface level areas of diversity give rise to a team's social identity. Research shows that diverse teams outperform homogenous teams, mainly due to the input of diverse experiences and perspectives. Diversity at this level allows for a rich and broad range of ideas.

At the other end of transparency is deep level diversity, such as values and beliefs, personality traits and psychological needs. These are not readily apparent and take time and care to discover. When well-managed, diversity at this level offers opportunity for extreme high performance in teams because members are able to delegate, collaborate and share tasks without fear of judgement. They also have the freedom to work according to their personalities and strengths, thereby tapping into vital sources of individual motivation.

In the middle area are the functional aspects of diversity, such as education and training. These areas become important to teams when it comes to structuring work groups to achieve tasks that require different skillsets. In order to build and maintain a healthy and highly functioning diverse team, time should be spent including diversity on all levels. This can only be done by understanding both the tip of the iceberg – the part we can see – *and* the huge mass of personality lying beneath the surface – the personality traits, the needs, strengths, beliefs and values of each and every team member. It's these hidden areas of diversity that give rise to the wealth of human intelligence within our teams and organisations.

When we're curious about our team members, we make an effort to understand the whole of them. That lubricates team efficiency through trust and builds authentic connections with each other. In doing so, we unlock the human intelligence of creativity, as well as team power.

Human intelligence helps us lay the foundations for self and team wellbeing. We build teams that feed trust with commitment, consistency and sincerity, which harvests the rewards of engagement, performance and innovation. We use congruent communication that aligns thoughts with actions and behaviours. We acknowledge and value the diversity within our teams. We transform conflict into solution focused power.

Connected to the World in Which We Live

It's possible that you've seen the term Anthropocene crop up with more and more regularity. In the same way that the Palaeocene era was the moment of glory for the dinosaurs,

Anthropocene describes a geological epoch in which humans are the main protagonists. It's widely believed that humans have become the single most influential species on the planet, and not always in a good way.

Homo sapiens are having an increasingly large impact on the earth's geology and ecosystems. As the planet is our life support system, it's important that we discuss business, politics and industry within the context of human impact; on the environment, on food and water supplies, pollution and health, population increase, climate change, political systems, and outcomes of technology innovation, such as surveillance and national security.

We are so Anthropocene-centred in our current approach that it's questionable whether we have pushed the planet so far that much of the negative impact is now almost irreversible. But encouragingly, there is are increasing movements in both governmental and corporate sectors offering some hope that we can begin to reverse some of the damage done.

There has been an attitudinal change over the past decade, and many believe that businesses, as well as governments, should be a part of the solution to the environmental and societal issues that countries across the globe are facing. A massive 74% of consumers believe companies could operate in a way that boosts profits and improves economic and social conditions for their local communities. (*See Edelman, 2018.*)

But while more than 80% of surveyed businesses recognise that purpose, including environmental and social protection, has a beneficial impact on growth, only 22% have yet to embed purpose into their business 'to the point of influencing innovation, operations and their engagement with society'. (*See Carol Cone, 2020.*)

But there are many positive signs. The B Corporation Social and Environmental movement, started in 2006 in the States and now has a global membership of over 4000 registered companies covering more than 150 industries in over 80 countries. All of these registered businesses are B-Corp certified. Their success is valued via five main criteria, including social and environmental performance, public transparency and legal accountability, as well as the responsibility to balance profit and purpose.

Thousands more businesses aspire to be B-Corp certified. And as this social and environmental movement gains momentum, so it gets even more weight behind it; weight that has the power to change organisational culture. The proof of this lies in the evidence than several large umbrella organisations, such as Unilever, now only buy B-Corp certified businesses, for example Ben and Jerry's. Such movements have wide consequences.

On 15 January 2020, Microsoft President Brad Smith, Chief Financial Officer Amy Hood and CEO Satya Nadella announced the company's plan to be carbon negative by 2030. There is a big move towards a human-centred, socially aware framework for building and growing successful enterprises – and companies not on this trajectory are going to be left behind. Larry Fink, CEO and Chairman of Blackrock, sums up the future normality nicely in his quote: 'Profits are no way inconsistent with purpose – in fact, profits and purpose are inextricably linked.'

What this proves is that everything is interconnected. All actions have consequences. All challenges offer opportunity. Remember the George Floyd riots that shook the States then spread around the western world in the late spring of 2020? The protestors started with demanding justice for all with their slogans 'I Can't Breathe' and #BlackLivesMatter. Even though there are countless examples of police forces across the United States 'taking the knee' in solidarity with the peaceful protestors, within days the demands had escalated to 'Defund the Police'. Organisations have the responsibility to put the value of people, of environment, of society on a par with the value of profit and personal wealth. Everything is interconnected.

A bat cannot choose to stay away from expanding urbanisation. Chickens do not choose to be farmed as if they were tomato seedlings. Pests and diseases mutate (and so survive) because it's in their DNA. Water and fossil fuels are finite when pitted against time. Global warming is directly linked to deforestation, pollution, urbanisation and agricultural practices.

As individuals, we can choose what and how we consume. As leaders we can choose what our organisations create. We are in control of our purpose and our actions, and we do have autonomy over our choices. We are but one part of a massive ecosystem that's so sophisticated that it can provide all that every living thing on our planet needs. It is beautifully cyclical, entirely sustainable and joyously giving.

Chapter 5

The Call for Human Intelligences

Cognitive Bias in Culture

WHAT DO YOU SEE WHEN you look at this image? Where are these people seated and what is above the woman's head?

Perhaps you see a family sitting indoors, and above the woman's head is a window showing the foliage outside. Perhaps instead you see a family sitting outside, under a tree. And the image above the woman's head is a window, but one

91

looking into a house not out of. Or perhaps what you see is a family sitting outside under a tree, and the woman is carrying a basket on her head?

There are many ways to perceive what we each see, but what's the same for all of us is that our perspective is intricately linked to the paradigms we've created to make sense of the world over our lifetime. Of course, these paradigms are useful, essential even, for helping us create a massive database of information that we can store in our brain and use to simplify what we experience to make it understandable. These paradigms, or ways of thinking, can also cause cognitive biases so strong that you see not what's in front of you, but what your brain wants you to see. In fact, your mind struggles with constant change because it's hard work for it to alter an image or paradigm and create a new reality. It's so much easier to reinforce the paradigm than to shift it. And it's for this reason that many of us avoid change.

However, change is a constant. And by training your brain to be curious, creative and connected to yourself, others and the world, you can face change with a sense of excitement and expectation rather than dread and fear. Embracing change builds resilience and agility and gives you the edge so you can innovate and invent in a world that's in constant flux.

Fellow creativity researcher, Luc de Brabandere and the author of *Forgotten Half of Change*, asks a very pertinent question: 'Do you believe that we can create new technology but use our current mindsets to make the world a better place?' I believe not. I think we need new mindsets and new paradigms for the future of work – and too, the future of our world.

Technology serves us well, very well indeed. It has made possible the impossible and over millennia it has improved our lives in so many ways, from helping us harness nature and feed a growing global population to making travel across continents not only possible, but possible in a day. It continues to improve lives in numerous areas. Technology is a foundation of innovations in healthcare, transportation, education, leisure, business and government, to name a few. But we must remember that the real creativity lies in the human interpretation of the technological possibilities and this is why it is so crucial to put human intelligence at the heart of everything we do.

Human Intelligence and Leadership

In every industry, leaders are being challenged. Competition is tight and there is a constant call to streamline processes and cut costs. There continues to be massive disruption to old business models as innovations such as outsourcing, the gig economy, crowd funding, open source software, etc. challenge the old business paradigms.

For the first time ever, many organisations now employ five different generations as part of their staff. Ranging in age from 18 to 80, this age diversity requires new approaches to human resource management and engagement practices. At the same time, globalisation is pushing the limits of international trust and communication management. What's remarkable is that technology has, to a great extent, been a central part of all this change.

Of course, technology brings many benefits to organisations both large and small. Now that machines are designed to do the work that can be automated, leaders can turn their attention to igniting the people-power within their organisation, rather than focusing on throughput. But there are many challenges in managing the joint demands of technological innovation and teams of people, especially against a backdrop of demands for higher profits and, in more and more cases, higher purpose too. In many organisations, big data and algorithms have ascended to become the top priority of many managers because they tell an engaging and alluring narrative of possibilities, but this is often at the expense of human wellbeing.

Leadership, as always, needs to come from the heart and appeal to the heart. Human-centric leadership is about envisioning a new future, creating a new paradigm, and sharing that mindset through human-centric strategy, human-centric values, human-centric models of thinking and human-centric processes. Leadership is about enabling individuals and teams to use technology while harnessing human creativity to reach a strategic goal. The three pillar human intelligences of curiosity, creativity and connectedness can help you do just that.

Let's summarise the key elements of these three human intelligences to give you a road map for assessing how you apply human intelligence when forming strategies and defining values, models and processes.

Curiosity – Open to new ideas

- Promotes a culture of inquiry, rather than defense, which allows for positive change.
- Encourages humility and listening with the intent of understanding.
- Creates the habit of lifelong learning, which enables agility and resilience
- Encourages compassion and empathy, and the desire to take action to improve the lives of others.
- Promotes diversity and collaboration across sectors and departments, unleashing huge creative potential.

Creativity – New ways of looking, thinking and being

- Builds agile teams with the ability to move fast and change swiftly to harness opportunity from change.
- Encourages risk-taking and turns failure into opportunity.
- Builds resilience and the strength to face adversity, overcome barriers and recover from setbacks.
- Creates awareness of which type of thinking to use in which situation for optimal creative output.

- Develops team members' creative problem-solving skills.
- Converts creative ideas into products and processes that delivers value.

Connectedness – To self, others, and the world in which you live

- Allows you to be your best self through self-management and self-development.
- Allows for authenticity, transparency and accountability to build deep levels of trust.
- Creates purpose and a shared vision of the future.
- Encourages collaboration and values diversity.
- Fosters strong bonds and open communication.
- Creates ecosystem thinking that promotes an understanding and appreciation of the interconnectedness of everything.

With that in mind, here are a few questions for you to consider about curiosity, creativity and connectedness in your work and organisation:

- How much are curiosity, creativity and connectedness embedded within your strategic goals?

- How human-centric are your organisational values?
- How well do your models of operation (be they business, leadership, management or thinking) tap into the wealth of human intelligences in your team organisation?
- How well do your organisational processes recognise the difference between techno-logical possibilities and human potential?
- What can you do to apply more human intelligence to your strategy, values, models and processes?

Space for Technological and Human Intelligences

It's not a case of having to choose between technological or human intelligence. It's a matter of knowing when and how to apply each one. At the age of 18, I worked in a massive factory manufacturing female-hygiene products. I was assigned to the pregnancy test conveyer belt and was responsible for the elements in the pack identified by the letters D and E.

As the pre-formed test-kit packet came slowly around on the conveyer belt, my task was to take product D and E (in this case two different coloured tubes of liquid) from boxes in front of me and place them in compartment D and E of the test kit. I did this for eight hours a day, five days a week, so I could earn money for a foreign adventure. I haven't been back to the factory since working that summer, but I am almost 100%

certain that the work that I and 11 others on my conveyer belt did then is now carried out by robotics, artificial intelligence and geospatial equipment.

So what skills are best suited to the future of work? Definitely those of flexibility, agility and resilience.

- **Flexibility**: constantly looking for ways to adapt, enhance, adopt and conjoin, to predict and prepare for future challenges. Flexibility allows individuals and teams to respond to changing circumstances and changing expectations.
- **Agility**: the ability to respond rapidly and positively to change. Agility allows individuals and teams to work collaboratively and creatively to solve problems.
- **Resilience**: the ability to reflect, to turn failure into learning and to come back fighting after a setback. Resilience allows teams to bounce back after experiencing problems and use reflection to prepare for future challenges.

These human skills allow for quick and decisive responses to changing demands. But we also need to consider the interpersonal skills of empathy, compassion and courage.

- **Empathy**: the ability to feel the emotions of others.

- **Compassion:** the desire to take action to improve the lives of others. (The combination of these two leads to win-win cooperation and has curiosity at its core. To be compassionate and have empathy you must be curious about other people. Truly curious. Curious with the intent of truly understanding.)
- **Courage**: to take a stance, to take action and to make change possible.

These skills are the personal and interpersonal capacities that result from nurturing curiosity, creativity and connectedness both on an individual and a team level. Equipped with a toolkit jammed full of human intelligence, you and your team are in the best position possible to invent and apply technology where it will deliver the greatest value.

A machine does not dream of the future. It cannot envision a purposeful strategy. Algorithms in themselves do not have the capacity to predict or hope. Artificial intelligence is incapable of being even remotely intelligent without human input. Augmented reality is far removed from world reality with its joys and sorrows, serendipity and spontaneity.

But all these wonderful technologies have their place. Some bring speed and efficiency; others ease of communication. Some automate while others simplify. Some save lives and others aid new discoveries. What they cannot not do is hope. And that human power of hope is crammed with positive possibilities.

I believe that the ideal organisation of the future is one where curiosity is considered an indispensable value, where questioning is the norm and exploration the key to unlocking innovations that deliver value and solve problems. It's an organisation where creativity oozes from every individual and where teams work collaboratively and in a self-governed way toward a common goal.

The ideal organisation of the future puts the spotlight on wellbeing because it has a higher purpose of improving society and the environment – and that puts humans back at the core of the business. It is purposeful, productive, beautiful and spends a great deal of its time developing and nurturing the human intelligences of curiosity, creativity and connectedness.

Bibliography and References

Books

Abraham, Anna, *The Neuroscience of Creativity*, 2018, Cambridge Fundamentals of Neuroscience in Psychology

Boyatzis, Richard, *Resonant Leadership*, 2005, Harvard Business Review Press

De Brabandere, Luc, *The Forgotten Half of Change: Achieving Greater Creativity Through Changes in Perception*, 2005, Kaplan Business

Carey, Benedict, *How we Learn*, 2015, Macmillan

Covey, Stephen, *7 Habits of Highly Effective People*, 2020, Simon & Schuster UK

Csikszentmihalyi, Mihaly, *Creativity: Flow and the Psychology of Discovery and Invention*, 2013, Harper

Csikszentmihalyi, Mihaly, *Finding Flow: The Psychology of Engagement with Everyday Life*, 1998, Basic Books

Davidson, Richard J., *The Emotional Life of Your Brain*, 2013, Hodder Paperbacks

De Bono, Edward, *Six Thinking Hats*, 2016, Penguin Life

De Bono, Edward, *Lateral Thinking: Creativity Step by Step* 1973, Harper & Row

De Bono, Edward, *Teach Yourself to Think*, 2015, Penguin Life

Frankl, Viktor, *Man's Search for Meaning*, 2004, Rider

Goleman, Daniel and Boyatzis, Richard, *Primal Leadership*, 2013, Harvard Business Review Press

Goleman, Daniel, *Emotional Intelligence*, 2005, Bantam Books

Grant, Adam, *Give and Take: Why Helping Others Drives our Success*, 2014, W&N

Gratton, Lynda, *The 100-Year Life*, 2016, Bloomsbury Business

Greenfield, Susan, *The Private Life of the Brain*, 2002, Penguin

Koustaal, W. and Binks, J., *Innovating Minds*, 2015, OUP

Kouzes, J. and Posner, B., *The Leadership Challenge*, 2017, John Wiley & Sons

Laloux, Frederic, *Reinventing Organisations*, 2014, Nelson Parker

McClelland, David, *Human Motivation*, 1988, Cambridge University Press

Pinker, Steven, *How the mind works*, 1997, Norton

Rock, David, *Your Brain at Work*, 2009, Harper Business

Staricoff, Marcelo and Rees, Alan, *Start Thinking*, 2005, Imaginative Minds Ltd

Articles

Anthony, Scott D., 'Kodak's Downfall Wasn't About Technology', July 2016, *Harvard Business Review*, https://hbr.org/2016/07/kodaks-downfall-wasnt-about-technology

Bakhshi, H., Downing, J., Osborne, M., Schneider, P., 'The Future of Skills Employment in 2030', 2017, Futureskills.pearson.com, https://futureskills.pearson.com/research/assets/pdfs/technical-report.pdf

Barsade, G. Sigal, 'The Ripple Effect: Emotional Contagion and its influence on Group Behavior', 2002, journals.sagepublishing.com https://repository.upenn.edu/cgi/viewcontent.cgi?article=1101&context=mgmt_papers

Berlyne D.E., 'A theory of human curiosity', *British Journal of Psychology*. 1954,45(3):180 191, https://psychsource.bps.org.uk/details/journalArticle/3679291/A-THEORY-OF-HUMAN-CURIOSITY.html

Cone, Carol, 'Engage for Good', 2020, https://carolconeonpurpose.com

Edelman, 'Edelman Earned Brand', 2018 https://edelman.com/earned-brand

Gartenberg, C. Serafeim, G., '181 Top CEOs Have Realised Companies Need a Purpose Beyond Profit', 2019 August, *Harvard Business Review*, https://hbr.org/2019/08/181-top-ceos-have-realized-companies-need-a-purpose-beyond-profit

Gottlieb J, Hayhoe M, Hikosaka O, Rangel A., 'Attention, reward, and information seeking', *Journal of Neuroscience*. 2014;34(46):15497–15504, https://www.ncbi.nlm.nih.gov/pmc/articles/PMC4228145/

Gottlieb J, Oudeyer P-Y, Lopes M, Baranes A., 'Information seeking, curiosity and attention: computational and neuronal mechanisms', *Trends in Cognitive Science*. 2013;17(11):585–593, https://www.ncbi.nlm.nih.gov/pmc/articles/PMC4193662/

Gruber MJ, Gelman BD, Ranganath C., 'States of Curiosity Modulate Hippocampus-Dependent Learning via the Dopaminergic Circuit', *Neuron*. 2014;84(2):486–496, https://www.ncbi.nlm.nih.gov/pmc/articles/PMC4252494/

Loewenstein G., 'The Psychology of Curiosity: A Review and Reintrepretation', *Psychological Bulletin*. 1994;116(1):75–98. https://www.researchgate.net/publication/232440476_The_Psychology_of_Curiosity_A_Review_and_Reinterpretation

McCarthy, Niall, *UK's Shrinking Navy*, 2018, January, https://www.statista.com/chart/12747/the-uks-shrinking-navy/

Rederman, Marian N., Clerkin, Cathleen, Connolly, Carol, *Leadership Development, Beyond Competencies: Moving to a Holistic Approach*, 2014, https://www.ccl.org/articles/white-papers/leadership-development-beyond-competencies-moving-to-a-holistic-approach/

TEDX Talks and Videos

Cleese, John, 'On Creativity', https://www.youtube.com/watch?v=bC-gBeQYHls

Robinson, Sir Ken, 'Do Schools kill Creativity?' TEDx Talk, 2006 https://www.ted.com/talks/sir_ken_robinson_do_schools_kill_creativity

Images

Zuzunaga, Andrew, 'Venn Diagram of Purpose', Zuzunaga, Andres. Proposito. 2011, https://www.cosmograma.com/proposito.php

Dr Robert Laws, *Cognitive Bias in Culture*

Websites

B Corporation: https://Bcorporation.net

Human Intelligence in Action

Alex works with government organisations, large Fortune 500 businesses, INGOs as well as Start-ups and SMEs. Her clients include American Express, Ikea, Volkswagen and Hewlett Packard. Public sector clients include FrontlineAids, UNDP, Ford Foundation and British Council. She has also worked with top universities across China, and primary schools in the UK.

Alex has a reputation as a clear, direct and engaging speaker and you can hire her to deliver talks, webinars and workshops around the topic of Human Intelligences, including:

- Unlocking Creative Potential.
- Creativity for Teams.
- Human Intelligence in Leadership.
- Curiosity and Lifelong Learning.

Alex is also an experienced facilitator and can help design and run your meetings and in-house training days. She offers workshops around the topic of Mindset and Skills Development, including:

- Transforming Conflict.
- Building Resilience.
- Visual Integrated Thinking.

For more information about Alex and how she can help your organisation to ignite its people power please visit The Yurt Academy website at www.yurtacademy.com.

Client testimonials

"A most enjoyable workshop delivered in a very engaging and informative way. Alex is clearly very knowledgeable in her subject matter."

"An excellent and inspirational workshop that is going to revolutionize how I capture and use data, and ideas to train, present, research and pitch to clients."

"You cannot imagine how much you're helping me on my journey."

"Alex is a brilliant facilitator - really made me aware of my potential to create great things, especially now that I'm armed with those fantastic tools."

"Alex knows her stuff. Highly recommended."

"A great talk, very well delivered, both with confidence and humbly, and with a natural ease and willingness to answer all questions that came up."

"This was very informative and clearly presented. I got a lot of information and ideas out of this session and am looking forward to attending more in the future. Thank you, Alex Pearson for an excellent presentation, it was brilliant!"

Acknowledgements

IN THE SUMMER OF 2019, I crossed the Pamir Mountain range of Tajikistan with two fellow adventurers Marieke Reichwein and Kate Clampett, and I thank them both for undertaking that journey at the centre of the world with me as it has been the source of much inspiration for my continued research on curiosity, creativity and connectedness. Many of the notions within the book are the result of years of lively discussion with people who share a passion for exploring and celebrating ideas, and I would particularly like to thank Alison Clarke, Anthony Willoughby, Bob Maddams, Catherine Pope, Diane Marks, Felix Heinzelmann, Filippo Cagnetti, John Biggs, Lucy Kynge and Pattie Horrocks.

A special thank you to John Glynn, Chris Peach, Sonj Bignell, Marcelo Staricoff, Saranzaya Manalsuren, Jamie Pyper, Jo Godden and Susie Bates for their invaluable insights into the application of human intelligence within organisations.

I would like to thank Bridget Rooth for her scrupulous editing skills in the early stages of the book. Also, my good friends James Lindsay, Sam Christie and Tim Clissold for reading the first draft and offering both a confidence boost and invaluable feedback. I thank Jean Wolfe for gently nudging me to write in the first place. A big thank you goes to Deborah Taylor, my book coach, who has offered honesty and professionalism throughout this journey. Thank you to Catherine Williams for her careful page design, and to Andy Prior for his cover design.

For Dawn Hutchings and Helen Guinness, I offer thanks for allowing me to experiment with my ideas to a live and receptive audience. Also, thank you to Nadia Aburdene for giving me the opportunity to share my thoughts, and experiment virtually, with diverse and international groups of people. Thanks must also go to John and Liz Thacker for welcoming me into their lively regular discussion groups.

Finally, I would like to thank my family. The origins of this book started many years ago and are the result of all the encouragement I have always received from my parents, Andrew and Joyce, to live courageously and to be whoever I want to be. For helping me construct my arguments I want to thank both of my brothers, Hamish and Adam, who also work in the field of personal and professional development and with whom I have spent many long hours chewing the cud on future strategies for training and development, and on adventure, mastery and insight.

About the Author

ALEX PEARSON IS THE FOUNDER and director of The Yurt Academy, and a lecturer in management at the Business School of the University of Sussex. Having studied Chinese and Literature at university, Alex moved to Beijing to study at the Central Conservatory of Music.

She stayed in China for 25 years, establishing several businesses and organisations, including one of the 'Top Ten Bookshops in the World' and China's largest Literary Festival, a theatre company, a choir, an outdoor management training company and a leadership training business.

Alex was awarded an MBE in 2009 and moved back to the UK in 2015. She lives in Brighton, UK.

Printed in Poland
by Amazon Fulfillment
Poland Sp. z o.o., Wrocław